WAYS OF WIELDING THE FORCE:
13 EXERCISES IN COLLECTIVE CARE & GROUP EFFECTIVENESS

Zainab Amadahy

DEDICATION

This book is dedicated to all those who teach,
mentor, role model and otherwise keep the wisdoms
alive..

CONTENTS

ACKNOWLEDGMENTS

Many thanks to nisha ahuja, Ashley McFarlane and Susheela Ramachandran for editing and reviewing a draft of this manuscript. Your loving support helped a writer living below the poverty line get her book out on time. I will forever appreciate your generosity of spirit.

Note: In this book you will see the use of s/he, her/his/their, her/him/them. While grammatically incorrect, this is my somewhat clumsy attempt to acknowledge those members of our communities that do not identify with either end of the gender binary. If anyone has suggestions on more appropriate pronouns, you are welcome to contact me at swallowsongs.com.

INTRODUCTION

"You don't do rituals because you don't have [anything] else to do. You do them because you have a lot of things to do, and because you want to do those lots of things very well. So life is seen as a mechanism that is supported by all kinds of ritual. This is why such a large portion of people's lives is invested in either recovering from ritual, doing ritual or thinking about ritual." Malidoma Some, Dagara and author of " "The Healing Wisdom of Africa".

"Native people believed they had to learn through contact or direct experience rather than through abstraction. Ceremonies developed as techniques for accessing knowledge." Gregory Cajete, Tewa author of "Native Science".

One day when I was on a panel discussing the relationship between "Love and Decolonization" I spoke about some protocols and ceremonies that are

2

used by Indigenous communities in struggle. These protocols are practiced to keep spirits high, deepen connections among community members and maintain focus on honourable and just outcomes. I noted that such protocols allow people to benefit from "good mind" and that there was an increasing amount of mainstream scientific research that demonstrated the many advantages of engaging in these and similar activities.

Because ceremonies and protocols allow participants to give thanks, vision an optimistic future, feel grounded on their land, connect to ancestors, feel responsibility to coming generations and cooperate together they generate biological processes that cultivate wellbeing. More than that, they generate results in terms of communities achieving their many-faceted goals.

Mainstream science is starting to understand that cultivating thoughts, feelings and actions based in generosity, gratitude, optimism, hope, compassion and cooperation are good for our physical health and mental capacities. Such states of being help our bodies heal from injuries or the impact of stress. They heighten our immunity, enhance creativity, facilitate problem-solving and much more. Of course, these biological processes feed into our relationships, affecting our friends, families and co-workers in similarly positive ways. Furthermore, the more you return to these feelings and shift your focus toward positivity, the more your body, including your brain, literally restructures itself so it becomes easier over time.

What's even more exciting, especially to social justice advocates, is the impact these states of being have on the outcomes of our work. New research devoted to assessing the impact of corporate leadership practices indicates that optimism and hope are more likely to result in desired outcomes than neutral or negative mindsets. While as activists we may not like the idea of corporations learning how to more effectively wield their power while generating happier and more productive workforces, there are still some lessons to be learned from the studies. But more about this later.

While on this Love and Decolonization panel, someone asked me if I could suggest processes that non-Indigenous activist groups could use to benefit from positive mindsets. I referred people to the science and challenged them to develop their own processes, noting that you don't need to claim a spiritual practice or be culturally homogenous to take advantage of scientific findings. Since then, however, I've thought seriously about that question and wondered if I might make a more effective contribution to the wellbeing of activists, community organizers and our movements

4

generally. Hence, "Ways of Wielding the Force", the booklet you are reading, downloaded itself into my brain.

There are so many great resources aimed at helping groups develop healthy and effective ways of working: books, articles, courses, workshops and so on. Many of these are, thankfully, free and easily accessible online. If we're lucky, we have people in our networks with the experience and expertise to role model and teach useful skills around organizing. These teachers and other resources help us learn about forming groups, visioning, setting goals, adopting strategies, implementing tactics, structuring agendas, facilitating meetings, organizing in communities, recruiting new members, long term planning, evaluating and so much more. These are valuable skills that activists, organizers and anyone who wishes to function in collaborative, community environments need to develop.

However, given that these resources and practices were developed within a framework of materiality, they often neglect a potentially huge variety of skills and practices that work on energetic levels to improve group dynamics and enhance effectiveness.

In my book "Wielding the Force: The Science of Social Justice" I shared emerging scientific knowledge that made the case for shifting our

worldview from materialism (that we live in a
material world comprised of matter) to one that
recognizes our inter-connectedness and inter-
relatedness on an energetic level. This worldview
recognizes that, at its core, everything is energy.

"Wielding" is grounded in cutting edge science and
ancient wisdom that is only now beginning to seep
into popular culture, the education system and
various other social institutions. This booklet
follows up on the new knowledge explored in
"Wielding" by providing some practical ways that
groups can take advantage of our energetic
relatedness to each other and the natural world.
These practices promise to make our work more
effective, more sustainable and more connected to
life.

As social justice activists and community organizers
we understand that knowing is not doing.
Theorizing is not praxis. Spiritual wisdom teaches
us the same thing. This is why we have ceremonies
and other activities that allow us to actually practice
our spiritual teachings. As we all know, praxis is
most effective when it is infused into our being; into
our every day thoughts and actions.

Through the 13 group exercises offered below,
"Ways of Wielding" will allow you to actually
practice the new/old knowledge discussed in the
first book. As we know, the more we practice, the

easier it gets because our body physically reshapes itself to accommodate what we focus on.

"If I destroy you, I destroy myself. If I honour you, I honour myself." Hunbatz Men, Mayan, www.whitebison.org.

These 13 exercises will allow you to develop expertise and skills in the following areas:

- Being aware of and better managing your thoughts and feelings as well as what energies you radiate into the world.

- Being aware of the energies that surround you, what is yours, what isn't and how to manage what is there.

- Catching story from non-verbal clues. Story is everywhere. It resides in our bodies, in the gestures and expressions of others as well as in the behaviors of plants, animals and the weather. We all know this at some level but we will come to feel it at a deeper level if we allow ourselves to develop the skills these exercises will begin to sharpen. Catching story enables us to respond to the life we're connected to in a way that promotes social justice and moves us all forward.

- Cultivating work and personal relationships that are mutually satisfying, meaningful and purposeful. There is no limit to how deep you can enter the cycle of knowing someone better and caring for them more. This cycle leads to some of life's most gratifying moments. Ask anyone why they do what they do and most of the time you'll get answers that range from making more money to catalyzing beneficial social change. But ask someone about their most memorable and meaningful moments in life and what you'll get are stories of connection – to people or other life forms. Healthy relationships are crucial to our ability to enjoy our life experiences. Which brings me to the final promise of how Ways of Wielding will help you practice:

- Loving and caring for others. Yes it's a simple act but, as we all know, very hard to do for everyone all the time. It might be easy to care for your children or your spouse but what about those who disagree with you? What about those who harm others? What about your own collective member who behaves badly? It's one thing to recognize we're all connected and interdependent. It's another to allow that knowledge to consistently inform your behaviours. I'm not one to suggest we can always come to one mind (a kind of consensus) over every issue or that we have to accept all behaviours. But we can always ask ourselves if we're acting in a way that is consistent with our values. We can ask if our thoughts, words and deeds are informed by our knowledge of what is most likely to create the better world to which we aspire. And then we can make changes, if we want.

If this all sounds New Agey and airy-fairy to you, think about the fact that science classifies our thoughts and feelings as nothing more than bioelectric energy. As we know from volumes of medical knowledge related to stress, our thoughts and feelings impact our physical wellbeing. Emotions that cause, coincide with and worsen stress include anger, fear, depression, grief, guilt, shame, etc. These emotions catalyze many reactions in our bodies: our biochemistry, brains, heart, organs and cells are all impacted. The longer we remain in these stressful states and the more we return to them, the more we jeopardize our health. It is now a well-accepted fact that stress is a causal factor in many, many illnesses. Certainly not the only cause, but a major contributor.

Changing our relationship to our feelings of anger, sadness, grief and fear can lessen the impact of stress on our bodies. In "Wielding" I discuss the difference between BEING angry and FEELING angry and how that one little change in how we experience our emotions can impact us.

Likewise the energies of positive thoughts and feelings have a positive impact on our bodies. The scientific evidence of this is quickly mounting but it is knowledge that the world's Indigenous peoples as well as many other wisdom traditions have had and used for centuries. The exercises/rituals I offer below are based in these knowledge ways and promise to radically alter the way social justice organizing is practiced. In fact, it should even impact our vision of what a socially just world looks like.

The suggestions I outline in this book are not going to replace the practical skills that help groups function well. They will not negate any of the "how to" resources currently available. However, they will enhance your work in many ways on many levels.

Furthermore, while my spiritual teachings have informed the activities in this book, you do not need to identify as a spiritual person or affiliate with any spiritual practice to benefit from the exercises. The activities are scientifically valid ways of enhancing productivity, effectiveness and a sense of connection within groups -- even in the mainstream. As mentioned, the new science is informing leadership training, healthcare, education and other activities in mainstream society. Although, there are some important and concrete differences between what I offer here and what is offered in the mainstream because I am not interested in shoring up a worldview or economic system that does not serve humanity, the Earth or Our Relations.

By definition and law, the corporate sector is about profit. Even not-for-profit groups are being pressured to prioritize financial goals over the needs of communities. New leadership training is still about motivating and inspiring people to behave and act in ways that result in greater profit for their employers. Even non-profits have to make the case that their work contributes in some way to maintaining and enriching capitalist society. Example: How many literacy, settlement service and training programs have to promise to make people job ready in order to qualify for funding?

Having reviewed some of the literature devoted to leadership training, I find myself concerned about the use of scientific findings to manipulate people's feelings and behaviours in order to make them happier about activities that not only enable others to profit from their work but also contribute to the destruction of the environment, the proliferation of consumerism and the depletion of crucial resources that contribute to the wellbeing of life on the planet. Training managers, executives and supervisors in techniques that improve their and workers' health and mental capacities will not resolve the fundamental problem of a financial system that is unsustainable and anti-life.

That is why I've written this booklet, which is more about addressing our collective physical, mental, emotional and spiritual wellbeing for the sake of healing each other and the planet on which we all depend. It's about enabling communities to empower themselves by heightening their awareness of connectedness and utilizing the energies of which we're comprised to raise the collective spirit and become more effective at the work of co-creating a kinder, healthier and more socially just world.

Social justice activists, community workers, teachers, artists, students and anyone interested in seeing their groups, collectives, organizations, relationships and collaborations achieve their aspirations will benefit by implementing any one of the practices I discuss in this booklet. In utilizing these techniques you won't need to look to "leadership" of any kind to manage, mentor, coach or otherwise manipulate you into contributing to the future of our communities. As a group, you'll be self-motivated, self-inspired and have the capacity to do that for yourselves.

For those who have read "Wielding the Force", this

booklet is a more practical set of activities that inspirit the knowledge discussed in that publication. In other words, this booklet is about taking action. If you haven't read "Wielding" you don't need to. Even without that information you will still benefit from incorporating these activities into your personal and group life. You don't have to be aware of how something is healing you to benefit from it. Why?

If you operate out of a spiritual framework you possibly already have an understanding of how Spirit works. But if you don't, and it certainly doesn't matter, there is empirical, proven science that explains how and why these exercises will positively impact your social justice and community work.

As explained in "Wielding", positive/ pleasant feelings and mental frameworks such as optimism, hope, gratitude, compassion, generosity and love generate the best indicators of longevity, physical health and mental capacity. Many studies have concluded that cultivating a realistically optimistic mindset accelerates tissue repair, heightens immunity, improves mental clarity, facilitates problem-solving and enhances creativity.

Hard science tells us that the more often, the longer and the more frequently you return to these states of being the more you enable your brain and other parts of your body to restructure themselves so that you can actually create a physical bias toward optimism and positivity in your life and work. In this way you can spiral upward. You feel good, your body restructures and functions to intensify that feeling, you feel better, your body heightens the feeling and on and on it goes. You can enjoy a state of optimism more often, return to that state quicker after experiencing stressful events and be less bothered by stressful occurrences in your life. But as beautiful as that sounds, it doesn't stop at the level of the personal. As you heal yourself you heal others.

There is an increasing array of evidence that shows us that one person's emotional state is contagious and, although there are many influencing factors, we can help each other spiral upwards. Additionally, how you interact with other life forms on the planet (plants, animals and other beings in the natural world), can also enhance your physical, mental and emotional wellbeing. Many examples of this are provided in "Wielding" as well as other places so it won't be reviewed here. However, at the end of this booklet you will find website links to research institutions that offer free, plain languages resources to help you understand the scientific findings and their implications.

By the way, this does not suggest that your

negative/unpleasant emotions do not serve a useful purpose in your life and work. Feelings like anger, fear, depression, grief and others have a role to play in a healthy emotional life. So-called negative emotions should never be denied, ignored or repressed. In community organizing these feelings can keep you realistic, grounded, practical, focused and safe. They prevent you from being too open and trusting, too naïve and optimistic, in situations where you need to be more critical and aware.

What's important to understand, however, is that the physiological processes of negative states of mind such as anger and fear are absolutely not compatible with those of love, optimism and joy. Contrary to popular belief love and anger cannot be felt at the same time.

Because activists sometimes reject this information I have learned to explore this concept by putting the science away for a moment and drawing more on philosophy. In philosophy there is a difference between emotions and temperament. Emotions are reactions to external events. They are temporary unless you dwell on them and then they become your "set point" or temperament. Your underlying temperament is a state of mind you cultivate over time, consciously or unconsciously. Your "set point" is the place to which you return after an external event has rocked your world. This is the

state of mind you generally maintain, until
something external knocks you off your centre.
Your temperament can be positive or negative,
caring and loving or angry and fearful, but there are
consequences for either and they are different.

Furthermore, you can change your temperament
over time and with varying amounts of effort.
Spiritual practices, if you engage in them regularly
and sincerely, will help you shift form a negative to
a more positive temperament. If you are not a
spiritual person, it can still be done through
mindfulness techniques that are explored on the
websites of HeartMath, the Institute of Noetic
Sciences and the Good Science Centre -- to name a
few. Neuropsychologist Dr. Rick Hanson's book,
"Hardwiring Happiness", offers a template for
doing this that is based in biology. There are other
scientific and popular books and articles that deal
with how to shift your mental/emotional "set point",
though you will have to take into account that some
are not necessarily coming from a social justice
perspective but are coming more from a corporate
leadership training place. Yet the techniques will
still be valid.

Something else to keep in mind about incompatible
states of mind comes from Dr. Richard Boyatzis
from the Departments of Organizational Behavior,
Psychology, and Cognitive Science at Case Western

Reserve University. His writings show us that when the brain is focused and attentive, we certainly get tasks done. This is the state that many theorists, academics and researchers find themselves in when they are noticing, analyzing and constructively criticizing. It is the frame of mind many activists find themselves in when researching issues impacting their communities. So this is an important mind frame, not to be confused with the mindset produced by chronic stress.

However, fMRI scans show that while in this focused frame of mind, the parts of your brain that form the "Social Network" are shut down. The Social Network refers to areas of the brain that activate when you are socially engaged with others, whether it is at the level of thought or action. The Social Network enables and intensifies empathy, compassion, kindness, cooperation and other pro-social thoughts and actions. You are also more innovative and creative when the social network is active so your ability to problem-solve becomes much more expansive. Your focus shifts away from the problem and you become more motivated by the outcomes you want to create; more inspired by the vision you hold. For example, do you see a difference between being focused on wanting to alleviate your pain (solving a specific, current problem) versus wanting to be healthy in your senior years (having a positive future goal you're working toward)? It's a subtle difference but shows up differently in the brain.

My point is that, while you need both the focused and social functions of your brain to effectively work toward social justice, they cannot be active at the same time. So you need to cultivate both mindsets in a way that doesn't allow either to excessively dominate or shut down. Balance is as important in this regard as it is in every other aspect of life.

Another key is to avoid getting stuck in negativity and certainly not to allow it to motivate your work in communities. While a hyper-vigilant and focused mindset helps you notice, analyze and constructively criticize what isn't working in our world, allowing yourself to be mired in stressful feelings and thoughts is detrimental to your health, your relationships and the world you aspire to create. While you should never repress, deny or ignore any of your feelings, being stuck in any of them is not helpful. Even the pleasant / positive ones. This case is made very thoroughly in "Wielding" so I won't belabor it here.

I also don't want to suggest that people who are suffering from a clinical depression or any other mental or physical illness need only shift their thinking to become well. That is too simplistic and also discussed in "Wielding". There are so many environmental and social factors that impact our wellbeing that shifts in thinking can only count for so much. But to the extent they matter it's worth trying in my experience. Also, mere thinking reshapes our physical bodies and how they function. So the more often you practice shifting your outlook to be more optimistic the more skilled and powerful you become at it.

In any case, there's another concept regarding stress called the "allostatic load" I'd like to briefly discuss here. This refers to situations where everyday irritations and annoyances that we all experience mount until you find yourself in a chronic state of stress - stuck in fight or flight. Even when you're not depressed or stuck in unpleasant emotional states you can, over time, find yourself being impacted by long-term stress. Studies suggest that the only way of countering this is to, first be aware of it, and secondly, intentionally engage in self-care that aims to repair the damage caused by long-term stress. These exercises are among many ways that self- and group-care can reverse the impact of the inevitable stress we're all going to experience.

Social "soft" science has long demonstrated what hard science is finally telling us. Many, many studies have shown us that the carrot is more effective than the stick when it comes to motivating people to do and be their best while co-creating a better world. However, not any and every carrot will do the trick. For example, research looking at how corporate leadership can best motivate workers concludes that "negative emotional attractors" like invoking the fear response (e.g., "if you don't improve your performance you'll be let go") only work for so long. Similarly, we can expect that people motivated by "do something or the planet will die" and "if you're not part of the solution, you're part of the problem" will only be inspired for so long to work hard for social change. We can further expect them to burn out faster as fear takes a heavy toll on the body.

Economist Daniel H. Pink's work shows that, once survival needs are met and a reasonable quality of life are assured, even financial carrots (like promised bonuses and raises) are ineffective at motivating people to work harder, smarter or with more creativity. And none of these motivators generates enthusiasm, optimism or cooperation.

On the other hand, "positive emotional attractors" or PEA's, as they are referred to in the literature, motivate performance and are more likely to achieve desired, sustainable results. An example of a PEA is encouraging workers to see themselves as contributing to some greater good, such as reminding your "team" that selling solar systems helps the planet. Or telling folks that a percentage of company profits supports cancer research. PEA's are a source of inspiration about the bigger picture and it seems from the research that almost everyone cares about contributing to the world in positive ways.

When achievements and results are measured, positive motivators produce improved AND sustainable outcomes. People work harder, are more creative, more adaptable and achieve better results. Additionally, although this is not necessarily a goal of the business world, the people doing the motivating, as well as those being motivated, transform to become more emotionally and socially skilled in the process.

What this suggests is that motivating ourselves with the vision of the world we aspire to create is far more inspiring and effective than acting out of our fears about worst-case scenarios. The more we can create images of the desired vision, with whatever we have available (words, visual art, music, role modeling, film, websites, etc.), the more likely we are to stay motivated and inspire others to join us in our work.

Pro-social emotions, thoughts and actions inspire and motivate more pro-social actions in yourself and others. These result in more optimism, generosity, cooperation, compassion, kindness, productivity and an awareness of inter-connectedness. Groups, communities and societies can benefit from an upwardly moving spiral of cooperative, kind and productive people. And before you know it, we'll be living in that better world we worked together to create.

This is how the exercises in this booklet can help your group, co-operative and community. They will enable you, as a group, to be more effective, produce sustainable results, enjoy success, recruit and retain members as well as minimize time spent on resolving tension or managing conflict. These activities will energize, inspire, motivate and generally lift the collective spirit while we transform our world for the better.

SPIRITUAL & CULTURAL TRADITIONS

"In Native American traditions, the word "medicine" does not refer to the pills or tonics we take to cure an illness but to anything that has spiritual power, and that helps to keep us 'walking in beauty'. Words can be strong medicine. Stories can touch our hearts and souls; they can point the way to healing and transformation. Our own lives are stories that we write from day to day; they are journeys through the dark of the fairy tale woods.

The tales of previous travellers through the woods have been handed down through the generations in the poetic, symbolic language of folklore and myth; where we step, someone has stepped before, and their stories can help light the way." Terri Windling, "The Wood Wife".

To help you understand how these exercises can be useful let me digress to talk about art for a bit. Specifically I'd like to explore 1) expressive art, 2) transformative art and 3) sacred art. Of course there are many definitions of these terms and others out in the world and I don't want to impose definitions. However, I will discuss what I mean by these terms so that you will understand how I use them in this booklet.

In the dominant society we mostly think of music, visual art, photography, film and other disciplines as forms of self-expression. In the left, we like to emphasize collaborative, community or other forms of group expression. Community arts or collaborative arts are often still about either combined individual expressions or expressions of ideas, feelings and concepts that individuals within a group share. Either way it's about expression.

There's nothing inherently wrong with self- or community-expression. Expressing oneself is healthy so long as it isn't violent, abusive or otherwise oppressive. However, the 13 Exercises are not about self- or group-expression. They are about TRANSFORMATION - change that enhances your individual and collective capacities. They are about entering into a kind of group ceremony that alters you at an individual and group level, hopefully bringing you closer to each other and your collective goals.

Although there isn't a clear line between expression and transformation, the point I'm trying to make might be illustrated by a story. If I go to an herbalist seeking a medicine to help me sleep and she tries to sell me peppermint tea I might be a bit confused.

"Will peppermint help me sleep?" I ask.

"No," she says. "It will help your digestive system. Valerian will help you sleep but I don't have any. I have too much peppermint, so that's what I'm selling."

In this story the seller has legitimate needs to get rid of her peppermint. Though I respect her need to sell, it's is irrelevant to my need for sleep.

Self and community expression can be transformative, for sure. But the goal is EXPRESSION. It's very egocentric and self-involved. Now I know that egocentrism in many leftist and spiritual circles has a lot of negative connotations. And the story above wasn't very positive either. We are always being told to overcome our egos and be more generous of spirit, more communal and so on. This may be a reaction to mainstream culture's glorification of individualism at the expense of communities and the planet. However, the ego isn't necessarily the enemy or something to overcome -- at least in my humble opinion. Maybe it is the ego that allows us to develop differences that enable us to diversify and take on different but needed roles and responsibilities in our communities. Sure, it's a struggle to keep your ego in check and not allow yourself to feel better, superior to or fundamentally separate from other life forms. Perhaps this ego versus a sense of oneness is a natural tension derived from being alive and consequently a source of our spiritual growth.

In any case, when I was a young mother, I found it interesting to see how many parenting resources note that a baby has no sense of personhood or identity and that part of my job was to help my child develop a healthy sense of self, where s/he understood her/him/themself as unique and different from others as well as worthy of love and getting her/his/their needs met. This process is celebrated in mainstream culture.

In other traditions, however, this process is framed

very differently, for example: Babies are born without a sense of separation. They don't differentiate themselves from other life around them and are closer than adults to the Spirit World. As they are socialized and their brain develops they begin to think of themselves as separate, unique and different from others. Sometimes because of they way they are taught and raised, they begin to believe they are better or worse, inferior or superior to others. Thus, there are teachings, ceremonies and practices (like meditation) that are introduced to help children understand how to balance their sense of self with the reality of their inter-connectedness with and inter-dependence on other life forms.

In indigenous lifeways and probably many others, a community is only as healthy as the individuals that comprise it and the community impacts the wellness of individuals. Both are important and need to be nurtured. Making space for personal and group expression is one way to do this. You definitely need to express yourself. Your community needs to express itself. But expression is not transformation.

I like to think of transformation as a process where your self-knowledge deepens while your ability to give, share and help others expands and the two are related/inter-dependent. You can't deepen your understanding of self without an awareness of how you relate to others. You can't cultivate and deepen relationships with others without deepening your level of self-knowledge and self-love.

Hence, we all have a responsibility to make space for each other's self-expression. (At least I'd argue that as an important social value.) But there is no guarantee that expressing yourself will push you to grow. It may. It may not. Transformation, however, requires pushing past your comfort zone, forging past social boundaries and growing or transcending from one level of knowing/being to another.

The difference between expression and transformation might be likened to the difference between giving your kid the gift you always wanted as a child verses giving a gift that is fun and educational. The gift you always wanted might or might not be fun and educational but the question doesn't matter because that's not why you bought it. In this case the gift was an expression of your own aspirations. You might love your child but you've still confused your needs with hers/his. The gift addressed your needs. If the child's needs were also met it was a happy coincidence.

Giving a gift with the intention of helping your kid learn and be happy is a form of expression that is grounded in both taking responsibility as a parent and loving your child. The gratification you get from this kind of giving is a sweet by-product. The relationship between you and your child is impacted, transformed, in the act of giving. You and your child both grow. Similarly you can be impacted, changed, in the creation, experience or use of a process (ceremony, ritual, exercise, etc.).

In the creation of transformational art it is possible to "inspirit" or "charge" the work with a spirit, energy or entity. You may not believe this is possible but to those who believe it is, this is a process that will enhance and strengthen your work. The group's creation, whether a physical item, a dance of movements, a collection of sounds or whatever will impact you collectively. We'll get to some science that explores this concept in a moment but for now let's consider the concept of "sacred art".

SACRED ART

"The symbol of wholeness, represented by the medicine wheel, is still being used in Lakota ceremonies today. The center where the 'X' crosses is considered the home of Tunkasila, Wakan-Tanka, God. I speculated, `If this is the symbol of wholeness, the symbol of the psyche, with Wakan-Tanka at the center, then Wakan-Tanka or God would be within you.'" Dr. A.C. Ross (Ehanamani), LAKOTA, www.whitebison.org.

"All the stones that are around here, each one has a language of its own. Even the earth has a song." Wallace Black Elk, LAKOTA, www.whitebison.org.

Sacred art tends to be about creative works that are tested in cultural/spiritual contexts over centuries and are meant to invoke specific entities, deities or energies in order to perform some function in the world. This kind of art is not well-understood or respected in mainstream society. Secularism and Christianity have both regarded the creation and use of sacred art as idolatry (the worship of objects). It has been misunderstood, devalued and ridiculed for centuries. Sacred art is about invocation (calling on) as well as an expression of Divinity. It embodies a spirit or energy that has power in our world.

In the Yoruba tradition, specific drum rhythms call on specific Orishas (deities/spirits) each of whom have their specific roles, skills, energies and areas of expertise. Drums, dances, colours and masks also correspond to specific rhythms and relate to specific Orishas. These ceremonial "tools" are used in concise ways to invoke or "call in" Orishas for work that needs to be done. Hence they fit the definition of "sacred art".

Another example comes in the form of Yogic Yantras. These visual artworks are specifically designed from shapes that are symbolic of particular concepts and have concise meanings. Creating, possessing and using Yantras in ceremony is considered a very serious endeavor because you are calling in energies, spirits and deities that have impact and influence in the world, as well as on your consciousness. The Sri Yantra tattoo on your ass or the Kali statue you found on your vacation in Nepal carry specific energies that impact your feelings, thoughts, words and actions.

In First Nations communities you will find that there are ceremonial or sacred songs that aren't sung by anyone at anytime for any reason. While all songs carry a spirit or energy there are special songs that are sung at specific times in concise ways for explicit reasons because they are recognized as having power. They heal, condole, imbue or otherwise act on living beings in the world. So they are considered sacred and anyone who teaches, sings or receives such a song takes on a serious responsibility.

For people who would like a more scientific discussion of how sacred objects function in the world, you might want to consider the work of a variety of scientists who are studying relationships between objects at the microscopic level. Researchers have found that each molecule in our world vibrates at a unique, precise frequency – a kind of molecular theme song. This chatter among molecules goes on beneath our awareness but of course our own bodies are part of the symphony. Recording and playing back the frequency of a particular molecule can initiate a chemical reaction. This is the case even when the molecule itself isn't present. The chemical reaction needs only the frequency of the molecule to occur.

This is the basis of how homeopathic medicine is believed to work. The idea is that the water, alcohol or solvent that once contained the virus or harmful agent no longer carries the harmful substance but only its vibration. Thus, it can provoke a healing or immune response in your body without you being exposed to harm.

Now I know that theories around homeopathy are quite controversial and still under investigation. However, even if it all boils down to nothing more than the placebo effect (the name given to a scientifically recognized mind/body relationship that gives rise to healing and wellbeing) it's reason enough to pay attention.

Other scientists are looking at the ongoing exchange

of energies that is constant among subatomic particles. Photons (particles of light) and other forms of energy are always, in every moment, being exchanged. Little "particles" of energy get created in these exchanges. Imagine a subatomic ping pong match and then think about how that works in a three-dimensional spider web, where every point of reference on the web, every string, every intersection is in constant communication sending signals out into all directions as they likewise receive them. We're not always sure about what that communication is about but you might want to think about your body in this regard.

We now understand that every cell in our body is constantly communicating with all other cells through chemical and bio-electrical signals. This communication coordinates the immune reaction, the healing process and many other bodily activities. The brain is not so much a centre of communication. Neither is the heart. The body is apparently much more cooperatively structured than mainstream science has previously understood.

There are scientists now working on the hypothesis that the photonic (light) frequencies the body (or parts of the body) give off can signal illness and injury. Likewise certain photonic vibrational patterns might be able to restore wellness. It's still controversial but a very exciting line of exploration that is consistent with Indigenous and other forms of knowledge that have relied on energetic/vibrational forms of healing for millennia.

I recently visited Rotorua, considered the geothermal capital of Aotearoa (New Zealand). Prior to the arrival of Europeans in the area, the Maori inhabitants of the region considered its many geysers, hot springs and crater lakes to be a source of healing. When Europeans arrived, they too found the land to be medicinal and evicted Maori from their communities so they could build spas and complimentary services for tourists and visitors to the area. In the early 20th century some European-descended doctors visited Rotorua aiming to determine if and how the sulphur-infused environment was good for one's health. They concluded the whole idea was a myth. The spas were perpetrating a fraud, they said. There was nothing about Rotorua's geothermal activity that was, in any way, promoting human health. As far as I understand, the debate is ongoing to this day.

Eventually, through the political efforts of Maori people, many of them were given permission to return to their lands. There are active communities again living in Rotorua and Maori have taken charge of the tourist industry, sharing what they wish of their culture and history and inviting visitors into parts of their communities while ensuring privacy for other areas.

While touring the Rotorua myself, I noticed official signs had been posted for my benefit warning me away from dangerous areas that erupted boiling water and hot gasses on a regular basis. These signs listed the chemicals that rose out of the geysers and gurgling mud pools surrounding me. One of the mixtures created by the gasses being coughed out by the earth into the air was nitrous oxide. If you read "Wielding", and even if you haven't, you might recall that nitrous oxide is also called laughing gas because it makes you feel good. Your body produces nitrous oxide when you feel joyful and well. The more your body produces the better you feel, the better you feel the more your body produces. It's also part of your sexual experience and the more nitrous oxide you produce the more likely you are to orgasm and the more powerful you experience your orgasm.

So, despite the smell of sulphur in the air, it could certainly be that the original Maori and later White settlers of Rotorua benefitted from the good feelings that nitrous oxide produced. That's the start of an explanation for how this area is experienced as "healing". If you dig deeper you might learn that the placebo effect is more likely to occur in folks that have high levels of nitrous oxide in their blood stream. Traditional Maori wellbeing, healing and healthcare practices relied to a great degree on the mind/body connection. This is an energetic connection. The bio-electric energy of your thoughts and feelings impact your body, healing it. That's what the placebo effect is: an energetic phenomenon.

In fact, since we now know that chemical reactions are caused by molecules combining and reshaping themselves, and that this is caused by the exchange of subatomic particles and that subatomic particles are actually energy at their core we can conclude that even chemical reactions are essentially, by nature, exchanges of energy.

So maybe indigenous knowledge and other forms of ancient knowledges are not just superstition and nonsense. Maybe our understanding of energetic interactions and how we are impacted by them has some validity. To insist that chemistry is at the root of wellbeing, illness and healing in our bodies is like maintaining that television brought you the movie you're watching.

It's true at one level but clearly without screenwriters, a script, director, actors, producers, various creative and technical crew as well as many others the story you're enjoying couldn't get told. Furthermore, the story you're enjoying was also made possible by a number of researchers, scientists, technologists and investors over centuries to create the technologies involved in TV broadcasting.

There is extensive communication among objects at the cellular, molecular and sub atomic level throughout our universe. Energies are transmitted and received all the time. As we know, energy is information. So if you can understand this you might understand how sacred art objects, designs, rhythms and other items can receive and transmit energy. You might better understand or at least be open to the idea that transformational art can absorb, contain and give off unique vibrations of energy that impact us, even if it is below the level of our awareness.

Isn't it possible that First Nations people who talk of sacred places on the Earth, where ceremonies are most effective, know what they're talking about? Could it be that songs that are sung, dances that are performed and the plants and animals involved in healing rituals might be interacting with us at the energetic level, supporting our healing and wellness?

As we discussed in "Wielding", energies intersect and sync up all the time. One form of energy may be more influential than another but usually when energies collide both are changed in some way. We know that heart and brain wave patterns as well as magnetic fields sync up among humans and across species. We can measure this now. Energy exchanges happen all the time, mostly below the level of your awareness. Yet they still impact you. So you might want to consider this when you encounter sacred art as well as when you create transformational art.

In any case, there is a huge difference between expressive and sacred art. Sacred art has limits, boundaries and prescriptions around its creation, form and use. While sacred art can be created and used by individuals or communities it is not about expression. It's about connecting to a spiritual realm in a specific way for a specific purpose. Hence, it is no wonder that sacred art is not known about or much respected in mainstream society, which devalues so many spiritual practices.

On the other hand, the line between "sacred" and "transformative" art is not solid at all. The creation, experience of and use of sacred art can certainly transform you and others. However, this booklet is not about sharing sacred symbols, rituals or practices. Rather I am offering activities that you can employ to catalyze and experience a transformation that will help you as a group work effectively together.

The exercises I share here are not meant to replace spiritual and cultural protocols nor are they meant to impose protocols that are specific to any one culture. These exercises do not contain community "owned" knowledge and I have done my best not to appropriate anyone's culture. The knowledge underlying the rituals outlined below is available to anyone through the World Wide Web, publications or open teachings and ceremonies. They are, furthermore, not tethered to or rooted in a specific cultural practice and can be adapted and changed to suit the needs of the group using them.

In our modern world, groups are very likely to be comprised of people from a variety of cultural backgrounds and spiritual belief systems. In pre-colonial Turtle Island, and probably in pre-capitalist societies all over the world, when communities were small, homogeneous and better aware of their connection to the Earth, there were cultural structures and processes that normalized and routinized self- and community-care. These practices furthermore called on mystical energies to help communities cope with life and move forward.

In today's world, what's left of our self- and community-care tools are taken out of their original contexts and often used to manipulate and control. Consequently, as activists, we tend to reject them. Also, because we are living in multi-cultural contexts, we don't always understand, trust or relate to practices that originated in cultures we're not familiar with. Finally, mainstream society denigrates and ridicules practices that cultivate cooperation, generosity and compassion. Instead it celebrates competition, the profit motive and consumerism. Consequently, there are many ways in which we have been severed from our cultural and other wellness practices or don't see their relevance to our busy modern lives.

When communities that have maintained their wellness ways, and are open to sharing them with others, we can certainly benefit. But there are many disincentives to such sharing, one of which is the threat of cultural appropriation.

"Many white New Agers continue [the] practice of destroying Indian spirituality. They trivialize Native American practices so that these practices lose their spiritual force, and they have the white privilege and power to make themselves heard at the expense of Native Americans. Our voices are silenced, and consequently the younger generation of Indians who are trying to find their way back to the Old Ways becomes hopelessly lost in this morass of consumerist spirituality." Andrea Smith, Cherokee scholar, feminist, activist, "For All Those Who Were Indian in a Former Life."

Hence these 13 Exercises are offered as a way of

complementing what people might already be doing in their cultural and community contexts. They are also offered in the spirit of creating common group rituals or protocols, unique and specific to the group, its vision and it's mandate. I believe there is room in the universe to create and nurture new ways of community building while honouring and implementing the many and varied old ways. Hence, these rituals can contribute to an ongoing and evolving process for any group.

WHY 13

Thirteen is not just an arbitrary number. While in the dominant culture 13 is considered "bad luck", it is a number that many others cultures and spiritual traditions consider significant, even sacred. At minimum the number 13 can be considered symbolic.

Thirteen relates to some of the rhythms, cycles and shapes found in nature. It's also a number infused with feminine power. There are 13 moons in a solar year. A healthy young female body menstruates 13 times a year (provided drugs are not preventing it). There are usually 13 segments on the shell of a turtle, symbolic of Turtle Island (how some Indigenous people refer to North America).

Thirteen is a significant number in the Flower of Life, a geometric pattern found in the ancient art, stories and spiritual references of many cultures. The Flower of Life contains the fractals (structural patterns) on which all of life -- even all matter -- is structured. The Mayan Calendar, much more mathematically accurate than the Gregorian one used in the dominant society, recognizes the 13 lunar cycles and divides days into 13 segments which are further segmented by 13. Calendars in the Muslim and Jewish traditions are also based on the 13 annual lunar cycles.

Thirteen is the sacred number of the Orisha Babalu Aye of the Yoruba Tradition. This deity represents sickness, healing and movement from stagnant situations. Thirteen is also the number of the Egyptian Goddess Sekert who manages transitions, cycles, and life changing lessons.

In Hindu funeral rites there is a 13-day mourning period and on the 13th day there is a ritual bathing of relatives and new clothes worn.

The number is similarly significant in math and geometry. A couple of examples: Thirteen is a prime number, only divisible by itself. The 12 bordering lines in a cube are all connected to the centre, the 13th point.

There are other ways in which the number 13 is significant, symbolic and/or sacred to various peoples around the world. It is not, of course, the only number of significance but it is the one I chose as a cut off point in terms of suggesting exercises to help your group further its work. There are certainly variations on these ideas offered here. Plus, many others can be developed. My hope is that these 13 suggestions will spur many more and that, when practiced, they will further our collective work to co-create a socially just society.

HOW THESE EXERCISES WORK

"[R]e-arranging the furniture so we are sitting in a 'circle' does not accomplish systemic or transformative change" Patricia Monture, Mohawk lawyer, activist, author and educator.

"Like the sun, life spreads its light in all directions … but if we want to make a fire we have to focus the sun's rays on one spot." Paul Coelho, "Manuscript Found in Accra".

You may notice that many of the activities

suggested below are structured around creating, recalling or cultivating the group vision. What is a vision?

Firstly, for those of you with strategic planning experience, you'll need to differentiate between a Vision Statement and the type of vision I'm talking about here. A Vision Statement in the corporate sector is about a short paragraph that summarizes what stakeholders would ideally like the company to be like in 3-5 years. Clearly, that will not be useful to us here.

In the community sector, Vision Statements tend to focus on the communities being served. The Vision Statement answers the question, "if we were to accomplish everything we wanted in 3-5 years, what would our community be like?" Again this would be encapsulated in a 1-3-sentence sound byte for funders, website, media, etc. Vision Statements in both contexts don't contain a lot of details but do create a generalized mental picture or idea.

For our purposes in these exercises we don't need a formal statement and we're not concerned about sound bytes or the length of the vision as expressed in words. We also don't separate our collective or group from the communities we work with. If you have a formal vision statement, it can certainly be a part of the process but, on its own, I suspect it is not sufficient for our purposes with these exercises.

What we are more concerned about here is focusing on a future that inspires, motivates and excites your collective imagination. We are making our dreams, fantasies and imaginations come true! The more details we flesh out, the better. The more we draw on all our senses, with sights, sounds, smells, tastes and tactile sensations, the better. As we formulate or recall our collective visions we are trying to create a focal point for the optimistic, hopeful, positive energies about our group's capacity to transform our piece of the world. Small, contracted, limited thinking just won't do. The bigger, more exciting and more comprehensive the vision, the more we're going to commit to making it happen.

How do we know? There are many studies showing that our ability to hold onto on a hopeful, optimistic future will more likely create the outcomes to which we aspire

Studies at Case Western Reserve University into leadership models have shown that the more managers, supervisors and executives can inspire and motivate, the more people want to use their talent, seek innovative solutions and adapt to change. What's more, and this is why corporations care, inspired and motivated workers produce results. In addition, what are called "charismatic" or "resonant" leaders that can inspire and motivate workers have brains that are more "coherent", meaning that the right and left hemispheres operate with a high level of coordination. This is called brain integration. As discussed in "Wielding the Force", the higher the level of brain integration or coherence the better our physical health and our cognitive capacity.

More of the science around this is discussed in "Wielding" but we can also see the impact of optimistic visioning in the health care sector. In one study, for example, a researcher found that diabetes patients were far more likely to comply with their recommended treatment (medication, diet and exercise) if they regularly visioned themselves as happy, healthy and well in the future. This single outstanding factor was even more important than the amount of support provided to patients.

This is how powerful visioning is. This is how powerful our thoughts are.

Consequently, all 13 of these "rituals" are about creating, enhancing or remembering your collective vision. According to the science, this form of "conjuring" is most likely to produce the outcomes we are struggling for in our social justice work.

KEEP IT REAL

"… the development of economies and the movement of vast numbers of people into the cities has not changed the essential connection between human beings and the earth that engendered them; it has only caused them to forget. When the people of a culture no longer remember that they are but a thread in the web of life on Earth, then they all become homeless." Malidoma Some, "The Healing Wisdom of Africa".

One caution I would suggest for your optimistic visioning is to keep it real. The vision needs to be achievable; otherwise your collective subconscious won't believe it and that will sabotage your efforts. I can give you an example of this at a personal level. Suppose I wanted to lose weight and I envisioned myself 100 pounds lighter in a month's time. Not very realistic, is it? Even a year's time might be pushing it. Even less realistic is if I were to imagine myself with longer legs and the youthful look of a 24-year old.

Of course I'm exaggerating. My point is that when we envision something where the stakes are high and it never comes to pass the experience is hardly pleasant. If you vision your partner, who has just been diagnosed with a serious cancer, living healthily into old age and it doesn't happen that can be devastating. It can even leave you bitter and pessimistic about the power of visioning and even about life in general, some studies show. However, if you were to envision a future where you do your best to ensure, whatever the outcome, that your partner feels loved and supported by you, that's another story.

What does all this mean to your group's visioning process? That's hard to say. As many of the Elders I've worked with have done, I'll consider that question an opportunity to tell a story.

One of the sagas documented in the film "Fierce Light: When Spirit Meets Action" by Velcrow Ripper is that of the South Central Community Garden in Los Angeles. Between 1994 and 2006, this garden, located on former industrial lands owned by the city, produced a substantial amount of food for 350 families. It also served as a source of training and education for city-dwellers aiming to live more sustainably.

The community was devastated when the city sold their farm to a private corporation. South Central Farmers Feeding Families refused to comply with eviction orders. They staged protests and occupations, even as bulldozers arrived to destroy their fields. Hollywood celebrities like Daryl Hannah got themselves arrested to bring attention to the plight of the community. In the end, the families lost their garden. However, in the course of their activism they were able to raise a sum of money that allowed them to purchase a larger tract of land in a newer, healthier location. The community gardening continues.

What can I say? Sometimes things don't turn out exactly the way you envision them; they turn out better. However, I believe it's important to the visioning process to have trust in your abilities, commitment and determination to make your vision a reality.

Based on my review of the literature on achieving visions, the general rule-of-thumb I use these days is to determine how much of the vision is under my control and how much isn't. If I want to lose weight, visioning myself in the body I aspire to is helpful. Visioning myself doing the things that will get me there is also helpful, such as eating healthy foods, exercising, meditating, walking in nature and so on. In these visioning sessions, I do my best to imagine myself enjoying my slender body or enjoying the process to achieving it. Furthermore, I use the idea of "feelingization" where I notice how my future body makes me FEEL, both physically and emotionally. As noted in "Wielding", the brain can't tell the difference between imagination and reality. Imagining I'm 50lbs lighter will enable me to benefit from all the positive physiological processes of actually losing the weight.

Many studies have found, for example, that thinking about exercising can reshape your body (and your brain) in the way that the actual physical activity would. Physical activity might achieve results quicker (some studies conclude) but mental activity alone is still effective. I cover this in Wielding so won't belabor the point here.

In sum, what I'm suggesting is that if your group is totally in control over whether it achieves its vision or not, focusing on the vision more than on the path to getting there are both very effective.

On the other hand, if you are not in control of your vision, it's still important to have one and revisit it often but it might be far more effective to allocate most of your time in favor what you need to do to achieve the vision. So visioning yourselves having successful activities and going about your actions in cohesive, effective and skilled ways actually facilitates the realization of the vision.

It's a matter of focus. If you are not in total control, focus on the path, the process. If you are in total control allocate more time and energy to the vision itself.

By the way, visioning does NOT replace the need for skills, experience and hard work. If I want to

49

lose weight I still have to eat well, get adequate sleep and exercise. I still have to work on the mental disciplines of unconditional self-love and self-acceptance. Your group will still have to continue all of the activities and learn all the skills required for you to carry out your work.

It might also be important to detach from the vision.

Once you've articulated your vision and affirmed your commitment to it you need to detach. I realize this sounds like a contradiction to everything you've read so far and I have no science to back it up. Only teachings. How do you do this?

Stand back a bit and accept that your vision is one of many possibilities that may manifest. You also have to accept that challenges will arise in the process of achieving your goals and affirm that you will do your best to get through them. In the larger scheme of things, the vision you aspire to has to be negotiated with those many other life forms on the planet. If your vision is life affirming, allow that to feed your spirit and inspire you without getting too attached to things turning out exactly the way you want. Leave room for your vision to shift and transform over time as you and your group grow older and wiser.

Another story, pardon the digression, comes from a time when a seer delivered a message to me from one of my ancestors. My question had to do with whether some recent and financially risky decisions I'd made were going to pay off for me in the way I'd hoped. The answer was not what I wanted or expected but it was, as it turns out, what I needed to hear. As the seer interpreted it, I was asking the wrong question. No matter what path you choose, no matter how solid you believe your decision to be, no matter how much you believe it is in alignment with the ongoing renewal of life, you will always encounter challenges, I was told. The question I needed to ask was, "Do I trust myself?"

The way in which I interpreted this answer had to do with my own conviction, my own commitment and my own belief in the "rightness" of the choices I'd made, even if it meant learning some hard lessons. Furthermore, it wasn't just about the "rightness" of it for me. It was also about how my vision served a bigger picture: my family, community and the Earth. Did my aspirations align with the creative forces of the universe? For me that meant committing to the spirit of the vision rather than the specifics of it. It also meant enjoying the journey along the way because staying hopeful, optimistic, generous, compassionate, grateful and open to growth were not only going to contribute to my happiness but enhance my chances of arriving at my destination.

To date there is still no guarantee that I'll arrive

where I want to be. And, curiously, my vision of where I want to be has shifted over time, anyway. So, I've concluded it might not be just about the arrival. It might be just as much about the journey. Perhaps there's no difference between journey and arrival. In any case, self-trust and commitment feels a lot better than indecisiveness and doubt.

I don't know if this helps in your group visioning process but it is what I have to offer, so take it or leave it. But deny the science at our collective peril.

DEEPENING CONNECTIONS

"... the more humans know about themselves – that is their connections with everything around them – the greater the celebration of life, the greater the joy of knowing, and the greater the joy of being." Gregory Cajete (Tewa), "Native Science".

Another feature of these exercises is about deepening connections among group members. Why is this important?

Again, if we look to the hard and soft science we can see that connections based in caring, respectful, trustful, open and honest relationships have their physical, emotional and mental benefits.

Consequently, the more the members of your group can connect to each other in positive emotional ways, the healthier you become and the more effective your work. Authenticity and sincerity are important in doing these exercises.

Can you stress yourself out trying to deepen relationships? Anyone who has ever been in a romantic partnership, has been a child or a parent, can answer that one: of course you can. As with every other relationship in your life you're going to have to decide whether the efforts to forge intimacy and closeness are increasing or decreasing your stress levels (and group effectiveness). You can't expect a complete absence of tension and conflict in any relationship. But if you're able to reframe the tensions as challenges that will build your spiritual, mental and emotional "muscles". You will be less likely "stress out" and more likely to benefit form the renewal and healing these exercises offer.

Integrated medicine expert Dr. Joan Borysenko has coined the term "stress hardiness" to look at how in framing problems as challenges impacts our mindset and chances of success. When you see yourself rising to a challenge and committing to an outcome it makes a difference in terms of your experience of the journey. While there are many things in this world you cannot control about whether your vision comes to pass, Borysenko suggests you focus on what you can control. Yes, there will be obstacles, defeats and failures along the way. It's good to understand, critique and acknowledge these. But not so good to allow them to steal your focus away from the tremendous power we all have to impact our world.

HOW TO CREATE OR ENHANCE
YOUR VISION

"The idea of walking to a mountaintop to seek and find a vision is used by both an individual and an entire people. The vision gained is shared with others as part of one's participation in the world and in the creative process of human life and of life on earth. Each person is important and therefore each person's vision is important and blends itself into either the construction or destruction of the world." Gregory Cajete, "Native Science".

Group visions are dependent on the visions of the individuals involved. The group vision comes after everyone involved shares her/his/their vision of the future you are working together to co-create. (Not necessarily in words.) But what if you don't have personal visions? What can you offer to the group's vision?

While what follows is a suggestion on how to develop a realistically optimistic vision, there is no-one-size-fits-all process for doing so. As with everything I write, take what is useful and leave the rest. I'm offering this process because in my work with communities I find that developing personal visions for activists and community organizers can sometimes be a painful and confusing process. I've facilitated many a group where the request for people to think about and reflect on their ideal world has elicited tears. In other cases, people simply find themselves unable to do it. Why?

I believe it is because the exercise requires you to get out of your head and into your heart. For folks that have been traumatized, which so many of us have, this can be a scary process. It is your experience of injustice and/or your witnessing of injustice that has set you on the path to work for a better world. That trauma motivated you for a while, perhaps it still does. Your feelings about your trauma, whether experienced or witnessed, served a purpose. Maybe they still do. Thus, painful and unpleasant memories often arise in the process of visioning. They are protecting us from being re-traumatized, frustrated, disappointed or otherwise hurt. We then have a tendency to focus on what we DON'T want and hope it will inform what we DO want. When that happens, past hurts and injustices will steal your attention away and hijack your thoughts and feelings. It's important to work though this before visioning.

First, I suggest some do's and don'ts.

Don't:

- Try to vision when you're in crisis or under pressure. At these times your focus should be on surviving or resolving your difficulties. Your emotions will be turbulent and unpleasant. You'll be dealing will fear, anger, anxiety, grief and so on. These are not the feelings that inform optimistic, hopeful visioning. At the same time you need to feel these feelings and get through them, at least temporarily, so that you are in a creative, hopeful state of mind. So, give yourself permission to tend to your crises and stressors and feel whatever comes up for as long as it's there. When you're able to shift your focus somewhere else you can try visioning.

- Don't rush the process. If you're under time pressure you won't be at your best. In our fast paced world we often forget that moving slowly

can be very enjoyable. Patience is its own gift.
Take time to enjoy the process and you'll
benefit in many ways.

- Don't try to develop a personal vision in the
  company/space/energy fields of others. You
  don't want the visions of others to influence
  yours or derail the process you're going
  through. You may be surrounded by wonderful
  people but you want this to be YOUR vision.
  You need to give yourself space for it to emerge
  organically and spontaneously.

Do:

- Give yourself at least a half a day and reserve a
  second half-day just in case you need it.
  Sometimes the first day is all about clearing
  traumas and that takes as long as it takes.
  Trying to jump into visioning when you are
  trying to quell feelings from past traumas is not
  going to work. Clear the trauma, give yourself a
  break (a couple of hours or a couple of days)
  and then get back to it. We'll talk more about
  this below.

- Find some green space or a space by the water
  (lake, sea, river, etc.) where you can be alone.
  If it's too cold or you can't find an appropriate
  space try seeing if there is a greenhouse or
  indoor garden that will do the trick.

- Get comfortable with the quiet of your solitude. Try to notice and align yourself with the rhythms of the plants and life forms around you.

- Notice your feelings. If painful or unpleasant memories arise follow these steps:

1) Breathe deeply for a few minutes. Try to ensure your out-breath is twice as long as your in-breath because this puts you into a relaxed state.

2) You don't have to name, judge, criticize or analyze your feelings. Just feel them.

3) Accept what you feel. It is what it is.

4) Notice where in your body your feelings show up.

5) Notice how that part of your body feels: is there pressure? Burning? Sharpness? Churning? Twisting? How intense is the feeling? Is it easy to tolerate or difficult? You don't need to answer in words. In fact it's better if you just feel it.

6) Breathe in and out of that part of your body for a few minutes. This means imagining that your stomach or your neck or some other body part is actually doing your breathing for you, taking breaths in and out.

7) Allow your body to do what it needs: tense

up, cry, shake, whatever. If you want to stretch, twist, jump, walk around a bit - go ahead and do it! You may have noticed that animals in nature literally shake off their traumas. Physical movement alters your biochemistry and your brain activity. Becoming active is one way to move trauma out of your body. (But don't turn to movement to save you from feeling. You must still feel what comes up.)

8) Notice if there are new physical sensations. Notice how they feel and where they might go.

9) Continue to breathe deeply.

10) Take a break. Have lunch. Go for a walk. Go home. Try again in a couple of hours or days to vision your better world.

"Indigenous people tend to approach emotion, and sometimes even pain, as a sacred thing because they think it means that something in the person is moving in order to let something else come in." Gregory Cajete (Tewa) "Native Science".

CONJURING YOUR VISION

"The more intense an experience, the more likely indigenous people are to leave it in the language in which it came rather than to discuss and dissect it with words. It is almost as if discussing diminishes what is being discussed. Villagers feel that words conquer experience, dislodging experience from its rightful place of power. So unless powerful experiences and ideas are addressed poetically, or with proverbs, people don't want to take the risk of losing in a fog of words what they have struggled so hard to acquire." Malidoma Some, "The Healing Wisdom of Africa".

When you come back to your space and feel ready, follow these steps to create your personal vision.

1) Take deep breaths, again ensuring the out-breath is twice as long as the in-breath.

2) Now go into visioning. First, focus on the senses. In the better world you are working toward what would you see? What would you hear? Taste? Touch? Smell? How would you look? Move? Walk? What would surround you? Who would you encounter? What would you do every day? What would your home, community or workplace be like? Who lives there? Who works

there? How do you interact with them? How do they interact with each other?

3) Ask yourself how this better world makes you feel. Feel the feelings as you name them off. Ask yourself why you have these feelings. For example, if the better world makes you feel happy, decide why. Is it because you love your home, your community? Is it because you enjoy what you do for a living? Is it because what you do for a living helps people or animals or the planet? How do those feelings show up in your body?

4) As you ask and answer questions, try to develop mental images of the better world you're in. They can be still photos, video clips or feature length films. Whatever works for you. The point is to flesh out the details as much as possible.

5) If you have trouble focusing at any stage in the process, ask your mind (or your spirit or the Great Spirit) to help you quiet your thoughts and concentrate. At the same time, don't be harsh on yourself. Maybe you should let your mind wander a bit and see where it takes you. Maybe you have a better visioning process than the one I offer here. Or maybe now is not the right time and you need to clear more trauma or just rest.

6) In the end, when you have something you feel satisfied with, draw, dance, gesture, hum, drum or sculpt that vision. You can use the objects in nature

that surround you to do this, if you like. Try not to verbalize or write anything down. Stay out of your head. Remain in your heart. Move or create a representation of your vision using leaves, stones, sand, sticks – whatever surrounds you. It doesn't matter if it's incomplete or wouldn't make sense to anyone else. It certainly doesn't matter if it meets any artistic criteria. It is simply your creation and it will have meaning for you.

7) Bring your creation home or offer it to the Earth or anything in between. Later you can, write your vision down in words if you want. Or you can make an audio recording. At this point you can engage in some thinking about what parts of your vision seem unrealistic and impossible. For example, is your better world on Mars? Have the trees turned to your favorite shade of pink? Does everyone in the world agree with you on every issue? Perhaps you should leave out the less realistic aspects. Or not. Your choice as now you know the consequences.

You may also find that your vision shifts over time and will be influenced by others when you share. That's okay. It's part of the group visioning process. What matters at this point is that you now have the seed of an exciting, inspiring vision that, once planted, will not only grow to feed your aspirations but those of your group as well.

PERSONAL PREPARATION & SELF CARE

"The Peacemaker used arrows to demonstrate the strength of unity. First, he took a single arrow and broke it in half. Then he took five arrows and tied them together. This group of five arrows could not be broken. The Peacemaker said, 'A single arrow is weak and easily broken. A bundle of arrows tied together cannot be broken. This represents the strength of having a confederacy. It is strong and cannot be broken.'" Peacemaker Story, "Haundenosaunee Guide For Educators", http://nmai.si.edu/sites/1/files/pdf/education/HaundenosauneeGuide.pdf.

"We are afraid to change because we think that, after so much effort and sacrifice, we know our present world. ... it won't give us any nasty surprises. ... to those who believe that adventures are dangerous, I say, try routine. That kills you far more quickly." Paul Coelho, "Manuscript Found in Accra".

We all know the old adage about a chain being only as strong as its weakest link. That's an unkind way of expressing an understanding that the energy/spirit that every person brings to the group gets incorporated into the group's energy.

This suggests that we take responsibility for our wellness and the energies we radiate.

This doesn't mean forcing yourself to focus on positivity when you don't feel it. What it means is investing in self-care that develops your self-awareness of what you're feeling, where you're feeling it and how you might be impacting others. Once you are aware of your feelings you can take responsibility for managing (not controlling) them.

Again, this does not mean you should feel pressured to shift your feelings. It only means that you offer yourself as much compassion as you would anyone else if they were suffering. It also means honouring your group process by doing your best to share your feelings, if not the reasons for them, so that everyone can be aware of the energies the group is dealing with.

Before you get to your group, however, you can incorporate some self-care rituals into your life to help you maintain your sense of balance and wellness. Remember that wellness is not about some static notion of perfect physical or emotional health. It means you have the capacity to respond appropriately (with kindness, generosity and gratitude) to the best of your ability, to your relationships. From this place of wellbeing you have more resilience and deeper reserves. These lend to the group's resilience and reserve.

DEALING WITH DISCOMFORT

"For me, forgiveness and compassion are always linked: how do we hold people accountable for wrongdoing and yet at the same time remain in touch with their humanity enough to believe in their capacity to be transformed?" - bell hooks

"People who love expecting to be loved in return are wasting their time. Love is an act of faith, not an exchange." Paul Coelho, "Manuscript Found in Accra".

Just as with personal visioning, it's not unusual for you to feel uncomfortable or distrustful of the power of the 13 Exercises. Not only are you vulnerable to your own traumas and the feelings they evoke, you are also opening yourself to what others in your group are radiating. While that is risky it can also be very satisfying.

I often think about the process as being similar to entering into a romantic life partnership. There are no guarantees you won't get hurt. In fact, you probably will get hurt, more than once. The question is, is experiencing the depths of love and intimacy, as well as the spiritual growth that comes from it, worth the risk? Most people in our world behave in a way that suggests the answer is "yes". I believe the same is true about connecting with individuals in communities - forming community. Of course you will be uncomfortable and vulnerable from time to time. But if you don't give your community a chance to be the balm to your wounds, you'll never know that joy. And on that note here are some tips for dealing with discomfort and trust issues that might come up for you.

The first is about creating a safe space at the outset. If your group has agreements, guidelines or protocols for your meetings and activities, these exercises are not meant to replace them. In fact, if you have group agreements about how you discuss issues and treat each other they may help you put these ideas into action. If you don't have group agreements and feel you need some, there are many resources out there to help you. Googling "group agreements", "discussion guidelines" or variations on the theme will illicit many examples that you can use as a template for developing your own guidelines/agreements.

Discussing ahead of time how you will handle individual discomforts and personal tension is another suggestion you might want to follow. You can establish contingency agreements around what happens if someone doesn't feel safe or if tensions arise between people. Will you postpone the activity until the problem is resolved? Will you take a time out and resume the exercise later? Will you allow people to opt out and opt back in when they feel safer? There are many other options to consider. All have their advantages and disadvantages but it's better to discuss your options before a situation arises. This not only makes the space safer but represents another challenge that allows your group to develop spiritual muscles that make you collectively stronger.

I also urge that individuals in the group think about issues of trust and discuss them if appropriate. Often trust is about people trusting themselves to manage their own feelings about what comes up for them. For example, there are some people I work with that I don't trust to do what they promise. A simple example: if my son promises to pick up the rice I need to make dinner tonight and he never shows up, much less brings the rice, I might get very anxious. This is particularly true if he has a history of not coming through for me and I anticipate it will happen again. I can't control what other people do or don't do. So I might feel let down if my son doesn't bring that rice home. I might get angry or disappointed or frustrated or resentful if I have to go buy the rice myself or cook something other than what I'd planned. More importantly, I might be hurt that my son seemingly doesn't care enough about me to be reliable. (This has never happened, by the way, in case any of my sons read this. It's only an example.).

Trust issues potentially run very deep. But I can save myself a lot of anguish in the above example if I trust myself. For example, if 1) I don't rely on my son to begin with or 2) I establish a back-up plan. Moreover, I don't have to take my son's lack of reliability personally. I might share with him my frustrations about his behaviour and listen to his response, which might enlighten me about deeper problems in our relationship or help me understand my son better. A discussion might also help me check my expectations. My point here is, again, recognize what you can and can't control and decide how you're going to manage predictable situations that might arise. And I often find that many situations are perfectly predictable if you're paying attention. Just as many times we can observe a couple and predict their relationship won't last, we can, if we're honest, apply the same scrutiny to the dynamics of groups we work with and make accurate predictions about what lies before us.

If there are trust issues already in the group, these exercises may not make them go away. In fact, they might do the opposite and intensify them. So individuals within a group must determine what trust issues might be there and how they'll be managed. If some or all anticipate that tensions will arise you can demonstrate a sense of trust in each other and enter the process with open hearts and good spirit anyway, knowing there are no guarantees but you'll give it your best shot.

When you are blindsided by feelings or tensions you didn't see coming, you can still have an agreed upon process for how to manage them. It helps to remember that you tend to get out of an exercise what you put into it. If you think about a life partnership for instance, you can pretty well predict what will happen if you consistently hold back your investment into that relationship; if you are cautious and restrained about expressing your feelings - or even feeling them. The same is true in group situations.

Now, of course, in situations where people are feeling a sense of panic or are seriously triggered by insensitive or even abusive behaviours, that's another matter. If there are unacknowledged power differentials being exploited that's also an issue. If that's the case, your group clearly has huge problems and these exercises will not enhance your feelings of connectedness and unity.

It also might be wise to consider what connectedness can and can't do for you on a personal level. If you're lonely, depressed or have other needs you hope the group can satisfy, you might want to check your expectations of these exercises. They cannot help you resolve problems emerging from deep life issues.

All things considered, however, you can sometimes trust the discomfort. Certainly it's easier if you are grounded and reasonably sure that you will manage what comes into your path but it's not necessary. One thing I've learned as a result of participating in many ceremonies is that if you want the magic you have to relinquish control.

In describing what happened when he presided over a grief ritual for north American men, Dagara Medicine Man and author Malidoma Some wrote: "To express their grief required them to move out of familiar psychological territory to a place where their sense of control faded away – a place where their vulnerability would emerge with all its terrifying effects." ("The Healing Wisdom of Africa")

When I went to Catholic school attending weekly

mass was mandatory. Every Sunday we sat through pretty much the exact same ceremony. We stood at this time, sang at that time and kneeled on cue. Back in the day priests spoke Latin, which I don't speak, so if there was any variation in what was said from week to week it was lost on me. Mass became a burdensome, boring waste of my time in a way ceremony has never been.

Every ceremony I've ever attended was different. Something new and interesting always happens in ceremony. And to benefit from the healing potential of ceremony I had to be open to what came my way. I had to acknowledge and accept my fear without trying to control it. Because I want to benefit from ceremonies I participate in, I have learned to balance a sense of cautious anticipation with an acceptance of uncertainty.

Now that doesn't mean I'll put up with abuse. But it does mean that I enter into ceremony and many other life experiences with an open heart, wondering how I will rise to challenges that present themselves and how I might allow them to change me. It doesn't mean I never experience fear or anger or distrust. It just means I accept them and enter the process anyway, aware that my control over the situation is limited and that I'll meet whatever shows up with a spirit of generosity and openness.

Again, in my humble experience, people who don't benefit from ceremony are those who either resist their feelings or try to control the process so they don't have to acknowledge their feelings. So please consider whether this is an issue for you.

PREPARING THE SPACE

"A ritual space is a place loaded with symbolism, capable of keeping the psyche focused away from the turbulence of everyday life. It must be a place outside of the ordinary, a place that looks and feels like an oasis in the middle of the desert." Malidoma Patrice Some, "The Healing Wisdom of Africa".

Despite not knowing precisely what will happen in a spiritual ceremony or ritual, there are always time tested protocols and medicine items that are essential components of the space and are used whenever challenges arise. In many First Nations ceremonies the four sacred medicines of sage, sweetgrass, cedar and tobacco always have a role to play. In many African indigenous cultures, ceremonial spaces contain items representative of the elements: earth, mineral, fire, water and life forms in nature.

There are also boundaries to the sacred space in which the ceremony or ritual takes place. A circle of cedar branches, salt or stones; the wood, stone or earthen structure of a sweat lodge and temple walls are examples. These boundaries always have symbolic gateways or actual entrances and exits: the eastern door of a circle, the opening through which you crawl into sweat lodge or the temple entrance, which is often specifically placed to observe spiritual protocols.

There are also certain places on the earth that are conducive to specific kinds of spiritual work. Some places support physical healing. Others support the connection to Earth elements and energy dynamics. Some enable people to transform in a right of passage and receive information about their role and purpose in life. Still others fortify connections with ancestors.

While these 13 exercises are not cultural or spiritual ceremonies out of any specific tradition, there isn't any reason why you cannot delineate the boundaries of your space so you can benefit from the psychological comfort of knowing a place has been designated and maybe dedicated to host your group for it's special process. It's symbolic, of course, but you can infuse meaning into the symbol and then it becomes something more.

Furthermore, there may be spaces that are of special significance to your community, group or work. There may be spots where great struggles were waged or victories were won. Your collective relationship to your particular space may contribute to the significance of what you are doing there.

To look at some emerging and controversial science on this issue, it might be enlightening to review one finding that has been published by science journalist Lynne McTaggert around The Intention Experiments.

These are a series of experiments involving credible scientists who are trying to determine if and how the intentions of a group of people can impact the real world -- from curing cancer to accelerating the photon emissions of objects to changing the behavior of water. We won't review the results of the experiments since nothing conclusive has been published by researchers. However, in one publication, which discusses how to prepare for sending out intentions during the experiments, there is a suggestion that the space you work in is significant.

What the researchers have learned is that there are subtle changes in the energy vibrations in areas of the labs or rooms where "intentioners" do their work – if they choose that space consistently.

Likewise, they have discovered these same changes in energies around personal alters, where people conduct their individual ceremonies and prayers. You can look all this up on line on the websites of The Intention Experiment and the Institute of Noetic Sciences. Among of the many questions that arise out of this discovery are "Can the energies we radiate alter the energetic vibrations of the space we work in?" "Do these energies facilitate our work?" My spiritual teachings tell me the answer is "yes" but scientists have not come to that conclusion quite yet. In any case, I'm sure there is no harm in proceeding on the assumption that the spiritual teachings of so many cultures just might have some validity.

If your group wants to proceed on that assumption I have a few suggestions. First, fill your ritual space as much as possible with plants. In "Wielding" we explored how even thinking or imagining nature strengthens the mind/body connection promoting wellbeing and positively impacting the electro-magnetism your body radiates. The science on this is clear. So being outdoors, in a space with windows that look out on nature and/or having plants in your space will definitely enhance the impact of whatever you do. Furthermore, the more you can enhance the senses with natural relaxing stimulus the better. Singing birds, the sound of a nearby stream and the smell of lush environments will more than do the trick.

Another suggestion relates to delineating the borders of the space with natural objects such as stones, potted plants, cedar branches, whatever you have at hand. It will help you feel you are entering a designated space that will interact with your group to aid your work.

CONSISTENCY

"… the maintenance and growth of a community is [not dependent] on corporate altruism or a government program but a village-like atmosphere that allows people to drop their masks. A sense of community grows where behavior is based on trust and where no one has to hide anything." Malidoma Patrice Some, "The Healing Wisdom of Africa".

My spiritual teachings suggest to me that there are at least two kinds of ceremony or possibly two components of ceremony support our wellbeing. One is to help us out of a crisis. If we need to get over a loss, deal with an illness or adjust to huge changes a ceremony can help us do that. Another use of ceremony is for maintaining wellbeing by giving thanks for our gifts in life. Some of us who are trying to recover our cultures usually have difficulty with the idea of going to ceremony when there is no compelling reason or specific challenges we have to overcome. To me it sometimes feels like going to church every Sunday just because it's Sunday and it's expected. But this, of course, is not the point of maintaining wellbeing and giving thanks.

Maintenance of wellbeing and thanksgiving can often prevent crisis and eliminate the need for a ceremony to deal with it. I've been a part of groups that have check-ins, games other types of activities that aim to foster connection within the group and avoid conflict and tension. Some of these processes work better than others. In my experience, unless there is a problem, most people don't take them seriously and don't enter into them with an open heart. Most people function with their masks on and their guard up and they have reasons I refuse to judge. I've certainly done this myself.

However, if I go to monthly Full Moon Ceremonies or seasonal sweats and feasts for the dead, I can't enter into them with my mask on and expect to benefit fully from them. As mentioned previously, I get out of ceremony what I put into it.

This can be said of the exercises in this booklet. While allocating quality time to spend with your partner is no guarantee your relationship will thrive forever, it might provide opportunity to grow your connection to each other. Spending regular, quality time with your kids is no guarantee that your relationships will be trouble-free, but it is an opportunity to demonstrate your unconditional love and affection, the greatest gift a parent offers their child.

There are many options around how often you might want to practice these exercises below and I've made some suggestions you can take or leave. Nevertheless, my recommendation is to allocate specific times to do them regularly. Some can be integrated into your routine meetings, activities or events. Others might only be useful occasionally, on a monthly, seasonal or yearly basis. It's really up to your collective.

You will, however, enhance your connection to the natural world, which is inherently healing and effective, if you schedule these activities to coincide with patterns, cycles and rhythms in nature. For example, if you do activities on every full moon, equinox or solstice it will help you notice these times and how they may impact you, your relationships and your work. Doing the exercises outdoors, if possible, will further enhance your connectedness to Our Relations and your awareness of their healing and calming influences.

On that note, here are the 13 Exercises to help your group raise the collective spirit.

EXERCISE 1)

CREATE A TACTILE COLLAGE

"But the Great Spirit has provided you and me with an opportunity for study in nature's university, the forests, the rivers, the mountains, and the animals which include us." Walking Buffalo, Stoney, www.whitebison.org.

There are many First Nations cultures that make use of Medicine Bundles. These can be personal bundles, clan / family bundles, organizational bundles, medicine society bundles and so on. There are many variations on how to create a bundle, what can be included, how to care for it, how to use it and how to put it to rest. I consider bundles to be sacred. They embody and invoke a spirit/energy that can help you or your group accomplish goals.

The same might happen when you Create a Tactile Collage. Hence, there are some guidelines around how you should go about this activity, which I discuss below.

Besides the benefits we've already covered, making a Tactile Collage creates, invokes and assigns a spirit/energy to your group, what it stands for and your collective work. It can be a visual and tactile reminder of your collective vision. It can hold energies or call in energies that help you work.

Here's how to create a Tactile Collage:

i) Each member of the group brings a small, light natural (found in nature) object that is symbolic or significant to the group's vision and work. Objects can be instruments, stones, shells, crystals, bone, claws, teeth, plants, representations of the elements … whatever holds meaning for you. You can use photos but not of people. You should ensure that the photos are on eco-friendly paper using eco-friendly ink. If you choose an item you created to express yourself, please make sure it is made from natural materials and that your motivations for sharing with the group are less about ego and more about uplifting others. Also, make sure you're willing to give up these items to the group's collective ownership.

ii) Before you bring your items in to share, please either 1) wash them in salt water or 2) allow them to be exposed to sunlight for at least a couple of hours. Call me superstitious if you like, but in my belief system, over their lifetime objects pick up and carry energies that vibrate differently than their original patterns. This step is a way of restoring that original vibration.

iii) Put the items into a cloth bag, skin bag, bowl, basket or container made of some natural material. As you place these items in the collage, speak of their significance or symbolism to your group and your work. You may want to tell a story to infuse meaning into your object.

iv) Discuss as a group how the collage, when it is finished, embodies or represents your collective vision.

iv) Cover or wrap the collage when it's not in use simply to ensure that items are not lost. This might also protect them longer from picking up on energies in the environment that might alter their vibration.

v) Uncover and acknowledge your collage on a regular basis. Review the meanings of the items. Add more items or replace ones that are wearing out. When you permanently take items out of the collage offer them back to the Earth. Options include burying, offering to water or sprinkling over land.

vi) Expose the items to sunlight or wash items in salt water about once a year. You can make a group exercise out of renewing and cleaning your collage. New group members get to add to the collage when they join.

vii) Allow the items in your collage to grow your collective identity, focus your energy and remind you of what you're doing and why.

viii) When dealing with a conflict or a challenge, take a moment to focus on the collage, invoke the energies and symbols it contains and reflect on the collage to help you get through your difficulties.

Below are some options around the making your Tactile Collage. You can:

i) Assemble a new collage for every meeting, once a month or seasonally. Disassemble it at the end of the occasion or interval. The advantage is that your collage will always embody the current energy and focus your group radiates.

ii) Make a collage that remains in the group's space (if you have one). It will add character and be a point of focus for the energies you want to guide you. Another advantage of having a more permanent collage is that it can hold your group's story and strengthen your connection to your own past as well as honour it. There are some guidelines around choosing a space for your collage, which are discussed below.

iii) If you don't have a space, make sure your collage is small and light so that one member of the group can assume responsibility for it, taking it home, caring for it and bringing it back for the group's use. For collages that travel, keeping it lightweight is key and can carry its own symbolism of spirit.

iv) With a collage that travels, members of the group can also rotate the responsibility for its care, on a weekly, monthly or seasonal basis.

As mentioned above, please review these guidelines when making your Tactile Collage. My hope is that it helps you have a useful collective experience while not trivializing or appropriating another's culture.

"Before we begin, I would like to ask you why when we speak you do not listen, and when you listen, you do not hear, and when you hear us, you do not choose to understand what we say. This is one time that I ask you to listen carefully and understand what we have to say".---Frank Fools Crow, Chief of the Lakotas in the 1960's, www.whitebison.org.

Guidelines:

i) Do not use sacred objects or symbols as I have defined them above in your tactile collage. Now I know there are folks who are fond of saying everything is sacred and they have their reasons for that. As I mentioned there is different thinking on what "sacred" is. So please review the above section on "sacred art". Unless you have been trained in a spiritual tradition you don't know what energies these objects or symbols invoke. Remember this is not about expression. It's about transformation. So your personal tastes or sense of aesthetics are irrelevant. It's about the group and its impact in the world. Remember the story about gifting your child? What you offer to the collage should not emerge from your ego but from your sense of connectedness and spirit of generosity.

ii) Again, unless members of your group have the training, do not mix cultural icons, ceremonial items or symbols. For example, unless you are clear on the energies they radiate, don't add a Dogon mask, a statue of Ganesh and an eagle feather to your collage unless you are clear on the energies they invoke, contain and radiate. If you are clear on what your object's energies are, share that and see if those energies are compatible with the energies of other objects being offered. Of course, this is only possible if everyone knows what they're doing and has had some training.

iii) Don't appropriate objects and symbols from cultures and traditions that are not yours. There are both political and spiritual issues around this. Politically speaking, Indigenous and other peoples are tired of having their knowledge and sacred objects taken, interpreted, misinterpreted, bought, sold, owned, used and misused by anyone that has the power to do it.

If I walked into your house and took something, even if it was from your garbage, because it looked cool or because it made me feel good, I don't think you'd appreciate that. Even if you sold it to me because you needed the money, it's still a question of power: who has it, who doesn't and how it's used. It's also a question of respect and if disrespect is a part of the energy your object carries why offer it to your group?

Please use objects from nature and review the suggested items above.

iv) Placement of your collage when it's not in use, whether it has a temporary or permanent home, should be discussed. Generally speaking, you wouldn't want your collage to live in a busy place where diverse energies interact. You should probably choose a spot that is quiet and contemplative. Likewise, don't leave your collage on the floor where it can be stepped on or kicked.

In some cases it isn't a matter of do or don't but more about what placement can add to or take away from the collage. The eastern direction, for example, generally carries the energy of birth, rebirth and renewal. The western direction is about ending, resting and death. Light and dark places also carry energy as do cold and warm spots. Is there a reason you might want your collage to touch the earth, be by water or sit near a window? Discuss this and decide what works for your collage.

Spiritually speaking, if you do not heed these cautions you could be creating tension in your group through cultivating contradictory energies, radiating negativity or not taking responsibility for your power and privilege.

While I don't want to generate a fear of sacred objects or invoke guilt around privilege, I still want to impress upon you that as you open yourselves to energies you become increasingly sensitive to them. Just because you own a hammer doesn't mean you can build a house. Furthermore, just because you own a hammer doesn't mean it's the appropriate tool for every situation. Please respect ancient wisdoms that have tested these processes for millennia, even if you don't believe or understand them.

EXERCISE 2)

FEAST YOUR ANCESTORS

" ... if I am truly connected to my community, that community becomes a form of immortality. For the Dagara people, death results in simply a different form of belonging to the community. It is a lesson from nature that change is the norm, that the world is defined by eternal cycles of decline and regeneration. Having journeyed adequately in this world in your life, you become much more effective to the community that continued you when you return to the world of Spirit." Malidoma Some, "The Healing Wisdom of Africa".

This exercise allows group members to share a part of their story with each other, strengthening your relationships. You may have to do some research within your family and this will have its impact on those relationships.

If you don't know anything about your biological ancestors, as in the case of someone who has been adopted, you can share the story of an ancestor from your adopted family.

Try to choose an ancestor you have never met. This

allows you to connect or reconnect to family members and stories as you seek information on your chosen ancestor.

This type of sharing can consolidate a group's feelings of connection across individuals as well as communities. As you listen and tell stories to each other, try to find something in each story that reminds you of the need for your group and the changes you are working for in the world. How would your ancestor have benefitted from the vision you are working toward? How do the feel now about that vision?

i) The feast begins when each group member brings in her or his chosen ancestor's favourite food. If you don't know her/his/them favourite food, bring in something they probably would have eaten because it was plentiful in the time and place where they lived.

ii) Set aside an Ancestor Plate and put a small sample of all the foods brought in for the feast. In this case, you can bring a photo of your ancestor or an item that once belonged to them and place it near the plate. Someone can be designated to stand up and extend a verbal welcome and invite (out loud) the Ancestors to join your feast. This can feel silly if you don't believe you're actually talking to someone but you can think of it as symbolic.

iii) While you eat together, take turns sharing a

story about your ancestor.

iv) When the feast is finished, someone again needs to thank the Ancestors for coming and let them know the feast is over. Again, if you feel silly consider it a symbolic exercise. Return the food on the Ancestor Plate to the Earth or to water. Please make sure that all food prepared for the feast is either eaten or returned to the Earth. Wouldn't it be consistent with your group's values to share any food left over with your local friendship centre or shelter? You might even want to plan for that by bringing extra.

While I believe that spiritual entities are nourished by the energy of the foods they are offered, this belief isn't necessary to benefit from the impact of this exercise. Symbolic or not, you will get to know each other better, probably strengthen relationships with family and deepen your own self knowledge - at minimum.

You can feast an ancestor of one group member per meeting or have everyone in the group do it together for a special gathering where no other business is done.

If you want to make the time and investment of energy, you can prepare the food together as your initial step, though from my experience you'll need a large kitchen and lots of counter space. You'll also need to coordinate use of the appliances.

Despite the extra organizing efforts, it can be fun. Or not, your choice.

Feasting the Ancestors can be a monthly or seasonal event.

Individuals can work with the same ancestor more than once, sharing a different story every time and deepening their relationship with that person. Or you can feast a different ancestor every time, requiring you to collect more stories from more of your living family members.

However you feast your ancestors do it with respect, generosity, gratitude and playfulness for the best results.

EXERCISE 3) CREATE A SOCIAL JUSTICE SINGULARITY

A mathematician coined the term Technological Singularity in the 1950's. It refers to the theory that a super intelligence will one day emerge out of all the technology that humans have created and render humanity as we know it obsolete.

I've chosen the name Social Justice Singularity to refer to a construct infused with the universal spirit of social justice that propels humanity to new evolutionary heights. What this will look like is up to the group to determine and may change over time and with the participation of various members.

The idea of creating a Social Justice Singularity (SJS) is similar to that of a Tactile Collage. With an SJS, however, you can incorporate larger, heavier items because you won't be travelling with it.

To create your SJS:

i) Pick a spot that won't be disturbed. Place a table or stand in the designated spot. You can also incorporate the walls surrounding your spot into the SJS. Review some of the placement advice for creating a Tactile Collage.

ii) As with the collage, everyone in the group offers something symbolic and significant to the group's vision of social justice. Again apply the same guidelines to your selection of objects as in the Tactile Collage.

iii) Everyone explains the significance of the object they give to the SJS.

iv) Decorate the SJS space with colourful cloths, artwork, candles, incense – whatever resonates. Recorded or live music is a nice touch too.

v) When you do check-ins, evaluations of your work, planning or are resolving group tension, gather around that SJS to invoke and enjoy the spirit it contains.

EXERCISE 4)

SPIRITUAL SHOW & TELL

"...when faithful human beings or other creatures call upon them for help, they [the Spirits of the Four Directions] must send their powers..." Fools Crow, LAKOTA, www.whitebison.org

This exercise allows you to bring nature into your group and work in a personal and heartfelt way. It allows objects in nature to symbolize your group vision or aspects of your group's story. It allows the energy of the object to strengthen your work and your connections to each other.

i) Each person brings an object from nature (feathers, stones, plants, herb, shells, bones, teeth, claws, sand ... whatever resonates).

ii) Share your a story about why the item calls to

you. Talk about how the item makes you feel. How does the item relate to your group's vision?

iii) Everyone passes their item to the right.

iv) With the new item in your hand see if it speaks to you, has a story or relates to your group vision. Share that with the group.

v) Continue to pass items along until everyone in the group has had an opportunity to experience all items and speak about them if they want.

vi) At the end of the session, when your item is passed back to you, return your items to nature or incorporate them into your SJS or Tactile Collage.

EXERCISE 5) CLARIFY AND CONJURE

"… if you believe in something, and believe in it long enough, it will come into being." Rolling Thunder, CHEROKEE, www.whitebison.org.

This exercise can be used prior to an event or special function your group is planning. The idea is to clarify your intention and call people into an event before it happens. Clarify and Conjure can also be used for sending out spiritual invitations to people to join your group. What you're conjuring is an energy that will attract like energies vibrating at the same frequency, so you will attract the people who will benefit from joining your group or attending your event while at the same time enhancing the quality of the event.

C & C allows you to identify what kind of person your group needs or your event would like to serve. It enables you to think about how people who attend your event or join your group will benefit from the experience. Furthermore, it prepares you to make an emotional investment in creating a sincere connection with people who participate in the event or join your group. It also may help you do outreach and publicity because it allows you to be clear on who your audience is.

The activity is mainly a verbal one but words have power not the least of which because they encapsulate our intentions and inform our actions. In a group context words can inspire, excite and motivate you to take sincere and heartfelt actions towards your common goals.

A) How to Clarify and Conjure for an event:

i) Discuss who might benefit from participating in your event. (E.g., students, young people, folks from X neighbourhood, women, activists, community workers, LBGTQ folks, organizational reps, artists, etc.) You can always cover any potential gaps by adding "any and everyone who can benefit from the event".

ii) Brainstorm a list of the ways in which participants will benefit. (e.g., raised awareness, better informed, new skills, etc.)

iii) Take turns answering the following questions with one word: How would you like people participating in your event to feel while they are there? How would you like them to feel after they leave? (Stick to emotions or physical sensations such as energized, empowered, optimistic, motivated, inspired, moved, calm, relaxed, etc.)

iv) Discuss the ways in which your group and the community you serve benefit if the event draws in the appropriate participants. (E.g., increased support, more donors, more volunteers, expanded networks, etc.)

v) Take turns sharing what action you would like people to take as a result of participating in your event. Stick to verbs. (E.g., give, show up, volunteer, participate, write, act, etc.)

vi) Take turns answering the following question with one word: What feelings will you have if your event is a success? Again, stick to emotions and physical sensations. (E.g., excited, hopeful, energized, uplifted, etc.)

vii) Close your eyes and take turns calling people out to the event using the words that have come up in the lists and discussion. (E.g., new skills, inspired, more volunteers, show up, hopeful.)

If you follow this process it will make a huge difference to the rate of participation you will experience at your events.

How to Clarify and Conjure for your group:

This process is a bit different but the underlying theory still applies.

i) Sit in a circle.

ii) Take turns to identify the kind of person your group wants to work with. Each person gets to throw out one word until everyone has spoken. Then if there are more words after everyone has had a turn they can be thrown randomly into the circle. (Eg. Kind, cooperative, eager, energetic, generous, optimistic, hopeful, compassionate, youthful, mature, experienced, open, teachable, etc.) Be as random as you like. Feel the words you are speaking and imagine them traveling out into the world and catching the right person's attention.

iii) Brainstorm the skills that are needed in your group right now. (E.g., social media, outreach, graphic design, public speaking, financial, planning, etc.)

iv) Brainstorm a list of how people who join your group will benefit. (E.g., make new friends, expand their networks, learn new things, etc.)

v) Brainstorm a list of how you want people who join your group to feel. (E.g, grateful, energized, excited, blessed, connected, confident, empowered, etc.)

vi) Brainstorm a list of how your group and the community you serve can benefit if the desired people join your group. (e.g., more publicity, larger network, involvement of new communities, more resources, new energy, youthful outlook, younger members, etc.)

vii) Take turns speaking out one word about how you will feel if you are able to recruit these people into your group. (e.g., energized, optimistic, excited, grateful, etc.)

viii) Close your eyes and take turns calling people out to the event using the words that have come up in the lists and discussion. (E.g., open, graphic design, new energy, excited, confident, etc.) Once again, be as random as you like and feel the words you are speaking. Imagine them traveling out into the world and catching the right person's attention.

For either version of Clarify and Conjure you don't

have to worry about whether you all agree in the brainstorming exercise. Why? First of all what you agree on will have more intensity than what you don't agree on. Secondly, in my worldview, you're not in ultimate control anyway so the Creator will send whoever S/he wants to send. Thirdly, your group will benefit from the involvement of a diversity of people. Finally, if there are limited opportunities (e.g., limited seating, vacant position) you will be in the rarified position of benefitting from overwhelming interest in your work. That can't be a bad thing.

EXERCISE 6) EMBODY AN ANCESTOR

"Death is not a separation but a different form of communion, a higher form of connectedness with the community, providing an opportunity for even greater service." Malidoma Some, "The Healing Wisdom of Africa".

This ritual allows you to intensify your connection

to ancestors, family members, each other and your vision.

i) Each member does research on an ancestor to whom s/he feels connected. In this case, DO NOT choose a blood relative or even one by marriage. You can choose a complete stranger. S/he doesn't need to be anyone famous or distinguished in any way. It's best to choose someone you have never met.

ii) Take turns to share a story or song, draw a picture, recite a poem, act out a movement or artistically express something about that ancestor for the group.

iii) Take turns to explain why you picked that ancestor and how s/he and her life relate to the group's vision.

iv) Each person calls on that ancestor, introduces her/him/them to the group and asks her/him/them to join with everyone else's ancestors to help your group work well together as you transform the world.

v) Always thank the ancestor aloud for her/his/their support.

EXERCISE 7) TRANSITION CEREMONY

This is a ritual that might help your group make a change. You can do this ceremony to ask for guidance in identifying the change that needs to happen and/or for guidance in making that shift.

A Transition Ceremony allows you to look inward and outward for guidance, inspiration and clarity around new directions; to recognize and acknowledge fears around change and call up a collective hope around the contributions that your group can make to the future.

Examples of when this ceremony might be useful: When you want to revise your vision, mission or mandate statement. When a long time member in the group leaves or passes on. When you need to shift focus and/or set new goals. When you need to resolve a conflict or decide a contentious issue. There might be other times as well and you will need to use your collective judgment.

How to undertake a Transition Ceremony:

i) Individually write down what you and your group are giving up, leaving behind and forgiving in order to make this shift and move forward.

ii) Share one or two thoughts from your list with group members.

ii) Fold the papers and burn or bury them together. (This can be done later if the space you're working in isn't appropriate.)

iii) Brainstorm a list of words that relate to the collective vision that you likely share around the new direction or changes that are to be made.

iv) Brainstorm your feelings about how that new vision makes you feel. Don't force yourself to feel positively or deny your real feelings. Acknowledge that you can have many feelings, some seemingly contradictory, about what the future holds. You can feel cautiously apprehensive, fearful and excited, sad and anxious. Don't judge your or anyone else's feelings. Just put them out there. If you can't articulate the emotion, share the physical sensation (churning, empty, blocked, heavy-hearted, etc).

v) Acknowledge aloud that all of these feelings and sensations belong to the group. Everyone's personal issues become a collective issue.

vi) Brainstorm the benefits of change in general. Don't necessarily think about the situation your group is in. Think expansively about the gifts encoded in transitions, renewals and shifts. Whether you like it or hate it change usually has some beneficial aspects, even if it's only about heightening awareness.

vii) Each person writes privately about how the

brainstormed lists make her, him or they feel.

viii) Each person shares one word from her/his/their list. Again no judgment. The word can be as cryptic as "the" or as charged as "terrified".

ix) Thank each other for honestly and courageously sharing your feelings. Commit to entering this transition with respect for each other's feelings and aspirations.

EXERCISE 8) EMBODY OUR RELATIONS

"Each creature has a medicine, so there are many medicines. Because they are so close to the Creator, they are to communicate that medicine. Then they bring help and health." Wallace Black Elk, Lakota, www.whitebison.org.

This exercise can help you connect to and honour the plants, animals and beings that provide us with food, clothing, medicine, shelter, transportation, teachings and even entertainment.

"Wielding the Force" explored several ways in which we are connected with other life forms on the planet and beyond. Even recalling or fantasizing about the natural world (gardens, forests, beaches) positively impacts healing and wellness. Thinking about nature and even imagining we are in nature creates a frame of mind that promotes physical health, mental clarity and creativity.

To Embody a Relation:

i) Think about an entity in nature that carries or exemplifies an energy/spirit that is significant to your group's vision and mission. It can be a specific animal, particular plant, a body of water, a wisp of wind, a drop of rain, a volcano, a tract of land, a mountain, a mountain range, clouds, whatever you feel connected to; whatever has meaning for you.

ii) Close your eyes. Be that being for 5-10 minutes. Imagine yourself as that mountain, cloud, waterfall, bear, ant, maple leaf or whatever.

iii) Ask that being these questions: What do you have to say to this group? How do you feel about our group? What energy/spirit can you offer us to further our work and achieve our vision? Is there a gesture or a movement you can offer us that will help us work better?

iv) Take turns sharing the words and gestures that

came up for you during this exercise. Don't judge what came up for you during this exercise. Don't be surprised if the entity/being you spoke to continues speaking even after the meeting. Don't be surprised if entities speak to more than one person in the group. Once you've established this relationship it may become an ongoing one.

v) Thank the Being for its wisdom and send it on its way.

In doing this exercise you and your group have initiated a closer relationship with the entities you spoke with. They will continue to communicate with you so long as you are open to it. Even if you think of this exercise as merely symbolic it can be an activity that gets your creative juices going and hones your intuition so you can be in touch with your own instincts around the questions asked.

EXERCISE 9) CEDAR CLEANING

In many First Nations communities cedar is used as a medicine that cleans and disinfects. The bark and needles have many uses from flavouring tea to staining wooden floors. A Cedar Bath Ceremony helps move energy blockages in the body that are causing physical or emotional illness. The energy/spirit associated with cedar is cleansing and healing.

A Cedar Cleaning can be used to clear a space of unpleasant spirits/energies, smells or memories. It can freshen the air and lift your feelings about a space. Working together to clean the space allows everyone in the group to share responsibility for the work as well as the maintenance of freshness and clarity. The movements alone are healthy and can generate more mental clarity and creativity when you sit down to do your work.

How to Clean with Cedar:

i) Assign some group members to collect fresh cedar branches and bring them to your meeting/working space.

ii) In the meantime, other group members can collectively sweep, dust, mop and arrange furniture in the space as appropriate.

iii) Once the space has been conventionally cleaned, use the cedar branches to brush the walls, floors and furniture in circular motions. Slowly and respectfully move the air around in circles.

iv) Once the brushing is done, walk through the

space, moving the air in circles. Feel free to sing, dance, play music, chant or chatter while doing this.

v) When the air smells fresh and is circulating nicely, put the cedar branches outside. Later they should be returned to Earth or water.

vi) Call spirit helpers, guides, Orishas, goddesses and ancestors into the space to guide your work. If you believe it is useful, ask your Spirit Helpers to remove any lingering negative spirits move off to a place where they can find peace.

vii) When you finish your work in the space, thank the spirit of the cedar and the tree(s) that gave of themselves for your benefit. Acknowledge and thank the ancestors and spirits you have called into the space.

EXERCISE 10) SOUND TAPESTRY

"Takes more than one lone voice to make a harmony; the harmonies of life weave wondrous tapestries; many tunes, many voices; melodies of gifts and choices." Zainab Amadahy, excerpted lyrics, "Lessons of the Peacemaker".

This is a very simple exercise that most of us have spontaneously tried at one time or another. Hopefully the intent behind this particular one will allow you to experience a new take on a "been there, done that" exercise.

When I wrote the song referenced above I was thinking about how music, enriched by resonance, additional voices, instruments and so on can serve as a metaphor for building community. While sometimes you want to keep the music simple, and that can certainly be pleasant, combining simple sounds can be very healing as most of us have probably experienced.

Sometimes community or activist groups can be surprisingly homogenous, though you'd think their politics would contradict it. I'm sure we've all seen this. So this exercise can be about cultivating a spirit of openness to difference whether in terms of culture and ethnicity, sexual orientation, abilities, age or whatever.

Working in musical realms requires us to draw on the right brain, as will this exercise. As we know from "Wielding", the right brain is pretty much neglected by most institutions in mainstream society. It is left-brained skills that are most valued.

However, awakening the right brain helps us think holistically, be more creative, solve problems and so on. So this exercise will help us tap into those skills. The only guideline here is to not form, think in or sing lyrics. Words are a left-brain function and though doing both does generate more brain integration, we want to focus on the right brain for this exercise.

Yet another point of this exercise is to coordinate and connect on a level your group might not be used to. You might find that your feelings and ideas about leadership, confidence, capacity shift as you switch from a meeting where words and intellect rule to a sound jam where other skills are drawn upon. That might be an interesting exploration into playing different roles in your group and empathizing with others.

An experience I once had in a ceremony was being the one people looked to when it came to leading musical components. I was younger then and had been quite comfortable just following the lead of the more experienced facilitator and her helpers. Stepping out of that role was uncomfortable and helped me think about the demands and responsibilities of leadership. It helped me develop more respect for such leaders and to recognize the capacities and skills that were needed to perform that role well.

There are a variety of other ways that this exercise might impact you. Open your heart, give it a try and see what comes up.

i) Breathe deeply a few times.

ii) Combine the voices in your group to give a Buffalo Yell or ululations or what some folks call the "Xena Yell". Do this three or four times on a count of "one, two, three," <yell>. This initial step is just to exercise your voice and get everyone vocalizing.

iii) In either a random or systematic way (your collective choice), one person at a time can start vocalizing. Hum, whine, make sounds, do a beat box rhythm, whatever calls to you. As each person chimes in try to compliment the sounds already out there. So you might want to harmonize, do a round, enhance or thicken the sound, whatever. Think of it as contributing to a drum jam only with your voice.

iv) Try to listen to the combined sound. When you're in a groove, stick with that for a time and see how it feels. Then someone can change things up. Every time that happens everyone else should change up to something complimentary. You'll probably go in and out of synchronized rhythms and harmonies but you can make a game of seeing how quickly you all learn to sync up and sound cohesive together.

v) Later you can include some non-vocal sounds. Use objects around you or on you to add to the complimentary clap, slap, scratch, scrape, rub, boing, tap, drum, step, whatever.

vi) Have fun.

This exercise can help you if you enter into it with an intention such as to be more open to difference, to stimulate creativity and/or to generate respect for all the roles that are necessary to the group's work.

EXERCISE 11) WISHING WELL

This exercise cultivates a sharing spirit among your group and puts out intentions that do good in the world. Water carries intention and as it flows, molecule by molecule, throughout the Earth, including in your body and into the atmosphere, it will carry your intentions with it.

In addition, as was discussed in "Wielding", more and more evidence is mounting that our thoughts and feelings have the capacity to impact the physical behavior of water. This is hardly news to many indigenous and other cultures.

The idea is that water can be healed by our thoughts and feelings and/or can hold onto the energies of our thoughts and feelings to heal others. With these intentions you can work with and through water to achieve your collective vision. Here's how:

i) Everyone bring a (reusable) bottle of clean, drinkable water to your circle, at least one cup.

ii) While holding your water, take turns sharing one wish for the group and another for the community/world/Earth.

iii) After sharing, each person pours a cup or so of their water into a common bowl.

iv) When everyone has contributed to it, pass the bowl around in a circle. One by one take a sip from the common bowl. If you are concerned about sharing germs, pour from the common bowl into individual cups. The idea is to share the water and the intentions within it.

v) As each participant drinks their cup of the common water, repeat your wishes and thank each other for bringing the water.

vi) Ensure all the water in the common bowl is either taken in by participants or returned to the Earth in some way.

At the end of this ceremony your energetic

vibrations will be changed and through the water within you the intentions put into the water will work through you – even if you aren't aware of them.

EXERCISE 12) CHARGE YOUR WATER

Moon Water is considered medicinal among many First Nations communities. It is made in ceremony, which I will not share, but I can share a process that allows you to inspirit or "charge" your water. There are many stories about how people have used Moon Water in their lives to accelerate healing. It can address illness of the mind, body, emotions or spirit. It can be used to accelerate the healing of relationships. It can be used to help heal plants and animals.

This ritual can take a while, so if you have a large group prepare for that. On the other hand, it's ideal for small groups. Here's how you charge your water.

i) All participants should bring a container of clean,

drinkable water.

ii) Sit in a circle with your water.

iii) Everyone in the circle names three things theyarge group prepare for that. ody, emotions

iv) Everyone in the circle takes their turn in acknowledging and thanking everyone else in the circle for some contribution they have made to the group. Again, be sincere.

v) For one minute, at the same time, everyone in the circle holds the container of water in their hands and feels grateful for it and all that it does for life.

vi) When that minute of gratitude is done, everyone passes the container of water to the person on their right and repeats the process of holding the container of water and feeling grateful.

vii) After every minute, for as long as it takes, everyone passes the container in their hands to the right. Keep doing this until everyone has their original water back in their hands.

viii) Take that water home, leave it at room temperature in a quiet place. Use it to drink, cook with or wash and see if you notice anything that arises in your relationship with that water.

ix) When you use your charged water, remember to send gratitude to those in your circle who charged it.

This exercise will shift your energy or the energy of those items and people that connect with that water. You might want to think about where to store your water at home and how to use it for maximum benefit. Again, even if you're unaware, the water will do its work. If you maintain an open heart you might be able to sense what it's up to.

EXERCISE 13)

FROM MOVEMENT TO CEREMONY

For groups who want to be physically engaged with the process of connecting to Spirit, here is a suggestion that might be helpful. It might also shift energetic blockages and awaken ancestral memories stored in the body.

Awakening ancestral memories is infused into the spiritual practices of many peoples. Even scientists, through the new study of epigenetics (how environment impacts genetic expression) are aware that we physically carry in our bodies the emotional impact of at least four and possibly more generations of ancestors. That is their emotional experiences shaped our bodies. And, as we know, our bodies impact our minds and emotions. So as we explored in Wielding, our emotions, decisions and thoughts are being influenced by ancestors we may never have met. This exercise might awaken those memories, feelings or thoughts and enable you to gain awareness, formulate questions or simply feel emotions that increase your self knowledge and contribute to the wellbeing of your relationships. Yes, the experience can be painful but if you push through that youo the wellbeing of your relationyour journey and your group will benefit.

In terms of the collective spirit, you are again bringing the spirit and energies of your ancestors together to empower your work.

Stand in a circle together.

i) Recall the vision of a better world you are working to create.

ii) Name the feelings and physical sensations that come with that vision. (Examples of what you might sense are buoyancy, groundedness, peacefulness, excitement, hope, tingling, goosebumps, connectedness, etc.)

iii) Take a few moments to each think of a movement, motion or gesture that expresses one thing you are feeling and sensing. (E.g., what gesture or movement would express a feeling or sensation you have at the idea of your work being accomplished?)

iv) Take turns contributing those movements or gestures to your circle.

v) After someone has performed their movement, everyone in the circle gets to perform it back to them.

vi) For people who have mobility issues, modify the movement for your body, so you are comfortable doing it.

vii) In sequence, one by one, perform your movements for each other, one after the other, connecting them together in a group movement.

viii) As a group, go through the sequence of movements, where every person in the circle performs all movement together. As a group, perform the sequence of movements as many times as you'd like. Treat the process as if it were ceremony, whatever that means to you.

ix) Once you've performed the ceremony as a group and have it down (more or less) take turns stepping into the middle of the circle and performing the sequence of movements solo. Everyone gets a turn.

x) Afterward, each person can share the meaning,

sensation and feeling(s) their movement expressed. Also discuss whether anything shifted in this process and how. Did your movements at all relate to ancestors – yours or anyone's? Did anything surprising, revealing or moving come up for you, share that with the group too? Did any memories emerge? There are no "right" answers to these questions. They are only asked to help you explore your personal and collective experience.

xii) Thank each other for sharing.

After this exercise you might note how the collective vision, the collective spirit, has infused your body and how it impacts your physicality from now on. Whether you are aware of it or not, your energetic vibrations have changed. Your group might want to set aside another time after this exercise to debrief what comes up long after (months) you have performed this ritual together.

CLOSING

"We forget so we consider ourselves superior. But we are, after all, a mere part of creation and we must consider to understand where we are and we stand somewhere between the mountain and the ant. Somewhere and only there is a part and parcel of Creation. Chief Oren Lyons, ONONDAGA, www.whitebison.org.

"The law is that all life is equal in the Great Creation, and we, the Human Beings, are charged with the responsibility, each in our generation, to work for the continuation of life." Traditional Circle of Elders, www.whitebison.org.

In Indigenous gatherings around the globe, the protocols are that if there are openings where spirits and energies are called into the space, there must be a closing to acknowledge, thank and bid farewell to these spirits. A closing also allows people to put closure to what they were doing, even if only temporarily, and switch their focus to the next task.

Closings are important. Most of us understand that fact. That is why we have graduation ceremonies,

118

wrap parties, final statements, funerals/wakes, etc. There are many in our society who advocate divorce ceremonies to help partners in a broken relationship heal themselves and move on. The need to acknowledge we have come to the end of something and are moving on to something else is a common human experience. That is why every culture developed an array of closing rituals/ceremonies for a variety of occasions. Closings give us permission to move forward, release pain, forgive or wish someone well before they move on. To me, closings are the exclamation point to a special gathering. They are the frame on memorable photograph, the savory spices on a nourishing meal or the kiss my little sons used to plant on me before they scurried off to bed.

These 13 exercises generally conjure energies, call in spirits, invoke ancestors and focus the group's attention around the vision and the work. At the end of the gathering it is important to acknowledge, thank and release those energies, spirits and ancestors. We also need to give each other leave to shift our attentions elsewhere.

Closings can be as simple as saying thank you and best wishes to all the spirits, ancestors and group members who have been present and focused on the tasks at hand. But you will get more out of the ritual if you can be specific about what you are grateful for. Just as when feedback and gratitude among ourselves is more useful than a generalized, "that was great", we do ourselves and the spiritual beings a favour when we itemize what we are grateful for. That way we communicate what we can do more of to support each other and the work while reinforcing and savouring the experience.

If you paid attention in the exercise(s) you'll be able to be very concise about what you're grateful for and to whom. What changed? What was strengthened? What new information was learned? What new skills were discovered or developed? What ideas landed? What stories emerged? How did you feel before you began? How do you feel now?

The 13 rituals can be modified to include more formal Closings or you can keep it simple. Either way, don't forget to do a formal closing of some type to mark the energetic shift that signals the end of this cycle and the start of a new one.

*****

On this note, please accept my heart-felt best wishes to you and your group as you explore the ideas I have shared with you in this booklet. May you enjoy your journeys as much as your arrivals. Peace.

RESOURCES

Institute of HeartMath

Institute of Noetic Sciences

Good Science Centre

ABOUT THE AUTHOR

Author, singer/songwriter, screenwriter and community activist Zainab Amadahy is of African American, Cherokee (Tsalagi) and European descent. Based in Toronto, she likes to describe herself as an "Indigenous settler".

You can find more of Zainab's writings, including FREE downloads at www.swallowsongs.com.

She welcomes any and all feedback.

CPSIA information can be obtained
at www.ICGtesting.com
Printed in the USA
LVOW13s1233270817

546569LV00011B/745/P